8/20

D1529149

PLEASE JOIN

The

CBD
SKINCARE
SOLUTION

About the Author

Dr. Manisha Singal is at the forefront of the cannabis movement and is an experienced conference and podcast speaker on medical cannabis. In addition to being a critical care doctor, she holds licenses to prescribe medical cannabis in Washington, DC, and in Maryland, and is a member of Americans for Safe Access, Women Grow, and the International Cannabinoid Research Society (ICRS). As a serial wellness entrepreneur, Manisha is the co-founder and chief medical officer of Aethera Beauty, a line of prestige skin care products featuring CBD and hemp. Currently, she is developing a technology platform to integrate Eastern with Western medicine.

Born in India, Manisha immigrated to the United States as a child. Her family settled in Pittsburgh, where she excelled at school, eventually attending the University of Pennsylvania. After graduating with honors, she attended the George Washington University School of Medicine, earning her MD and heading several research projects. She completed her residency at Georgetown University. In 2005, she accepted the position of chief medical officer at Specialty Hospitals of Washington (now BridgePoint Healthcare). Manisha currently serves as its chief medical officer, president of the medical staff, and as a member of the Governing Board. Since 2002, she has also enjoyed serving as a member of the Medical Director Forum for the DC Hospital Association.

MANISHA SINGAL, MD

The CBD

SKINCARE SOLUTION

· · · ·

the Power *of*
CANNABIDIOL
for Healthy Skin

Llewellyn Publications
Woodbury, Minnesota

FIRST EDITION
First Printing, 2020

Book design by Samantha Penn
Cover design by Shira Atakpu

Llewellyn Publications is a registered trademark of Llewellyn Worldwide Ltd.

Library of Congress Cataloging-in-Publication Data
Names: Singal, Manisha, author.
Title: The CBD skincare solution : the power of cannabidiol for healthy
  skin / Manisha Singal.
Description: First edition. | Woodbury, Minnesota : Llewellyn Publications,
  2020. | Includes bibliographical references. | Summary: "Manisha Singal,
  MD presents a comprehensive explanation of what CBD is and isn't, where
  it comes from, and how it works. This book features a history of CBD
  oil, common skin diseases and how CBD may help them, how CBD oil helps
  fight skin aging, and detailed advice on buying CBD-infused products"—
  Provided by publisher.
Identifiers: LCCN 2020010684 (print) | LCCN 2020010685 (ebook) | ISBN
  9780738764887 (paperback) | ISBN 9780738764948 (ebook)
Subjects: LCSH: Skin—Diseases—Alternative treatment—Popular works. |
  Skin—Care and hygiene—Popular works. | Cannabinoids—Therapeutic
  use—Popular works.
Classification: LCC RL85 .S45 2020 (print) | LCC RL85 (ebook) | DDC
  616.5/06--dc23
LC record available at https://lccn.loc.gov/2020010684
LC ebook record available at https://lccn.loc.gov/2020010685

Llewellyn Publications
A Division of Llewellyn Worldwide Ltd.
2143 Wooddale Drive
Woodbury, MN 55125-2989
www.llewellyn.com

Printed in the United States of America

To my best friend and husband,
Rengan

CONTENTS

INTRODUCTION

AS A CRITICAL CARE physician, I spend my days caring for sick patients. I see a lot of suffering, but I also get a lot of satisfaction from using my medical training and scientific knowledge to help people.

That's why I wrote this book. People are needlessly suffering from skin conditions that could be treated with the use of cannabidiol, better known as CBD. Skin conditions are not as dire as some of the trauma that I see in the hospital, but their itching, pain, and embarrassment can negatively affect a person's life.

It's not just the itching and pain, both of which CBD is uniquely suited to combat. Skin conditions also cause secondary psychological trauma. If you have ever dealt with a serious outbreak of psoriasis in a highly visible area of your body, or some other skin condition, you know the humiliation of having someone step away from you in line at a coffee shop. It's difficult for anybody to look in the mirror and feel happy and content when what they see is an angry red rash with flaking skin and scratch marks.

I suffered from a severe skin condition that caused extreme pain and embarrassment until CBD gave me the ultimate relief I was seeking. My health journey led others I know to try CBD, and they also had their lives changed for the better. That made me want to know more, so I decided to dig in and learn as much as I could about CBD. I came to the study of CBD with a lot of training in science and medicine. I graduated from the George Washington University School of Medicine and Health Sciences and did my residency at Georgetown. Then I founded my own practice and became a hospital's chief medical officer. This book doesn't get sucked into the hype about CBD; rather, it focuses on the science. There is a vast amount of research about CBD, and it's an area of study that is rapidly growing. As I scoured the medical journals, I discovered dozens of studies showing the positive effects of CBD. I also spoke to researchers, and they explained the way CBD is transforming the way we think about treatment for many ailments.

My personal experience and subsequent discovery of the science and research into CBD compelled me to write this book. I wanted to get the word out and help others who were struggling with similar skin conditions. Beyond that, I want to be part of the medical vanguard opening the door to all kinds of uses for CBD and medical cannabis. I believe, and the evidence shows, that CBD's powerful curative properties were key to my recovery. I am convinced that this amazing cannabinoid can be an incredible medical and beauty resource.

I could have focused this book more broadly on general health concerns because there are wide applications for CBD. But we don't all have migraines or chronic pain. We do all have skin that needs regular maintenance and healing. The skin is the body's largest and most visible organ. CBD is an ideal multi-purpose tool to care for it.

This book is a soup-to-nuts reference for using CBD in skincare. You will find a comprehensive explanation of what CBD is and isn't, where it comes from, and how it works. I've also included a breakdown of common skin diseases. Some are particular to skin—such as acne—and others can manifest symptoms on the skin, like arthritis. I've made recommendations for how to use CBD to treat each one, including dosage advice. These are based on my experience as a patient, a doctor, and a wellness entrepreneur. As someone who suffered a debilitating skin condition and realized relief with the help of CBD, it seemed only natural that I'd increase my professional knowledge of this compound. Those experiences ultimately led me to develop my own line of CBD products. My belief in the potential of cannabinoids like CBD inspired me to become accredited in both Maryland and the District of Columbia in the use of medical cannabis. That training gives me a unique window into the latest research and treatment options.

An important disclaimer: This book does not replace the advice readers should be getting from their own medical doctors. In addition, CBD should not replace the medical treatment they need or any medication they've been prescribed. My recommendations are general, so they will not apply to everyone. Readers should approach the use of CBD with the same common sense they would apply to any other health practice. Also, there are a lot of times in this book where I will tell you what the research shows and what it does not show. It's important that we don't get so caught up in the excitement about CBD that we ignore or go beyond the evidence.

Our skin is about much more than just the absence of disease. It also represents how we look and feel, and we all want to look younger and more attractive. That's why I also included chapters on CBD's role in keeping skin attractive and fighting aging.

Lastly, you need to be an informed shopper to buy the best products in the chaotic CBD marketplace. I close this book with a quick-and-easy guide to buying the best CBD-infused beauty products. These tips can also apply to other CBD products, from plain supplements to exotic products like CBD-infused chocolates and seltzer.

I've organized the book to be read from beginning to end, but use it in the way that works for you. If you're not as interested in the history, chemistry, and physiology of CBD, jump to the more practical chapters. You'll also notice that I barely touch on the stigma that's historically been associated with marijuana and tangentially with CBD. The science has moved beyond a lot of those arguments, and they aren't relevant to this subject, so that's not my focus.

I've seen the issue of alternative therapies and CBD from both sides of the healthcare divide. I'm struck by the way the medical research backs up my personal experience with the healing power of CBD. It's my hope that this book helps you discover it and understand it too.

1 · THE CBD MIRACLE

IN THE SUMMER OF 2017, I was excited to be going to a wedding. Most of my friends were already married, so I hadn't been to a wedding in a long time, and I knew it was going to be fun. I had just the dress for the occasion, and I wanted to have my hair colored and styled to do the dress justice. Like so many women, I regularly color my hair. After I hit my forties, a few gray hairs crept in, so it was nice to restore the luster and rich black hue of youth. I went to my regular beauty salon with my favorite stylist and followed a routine I had gone through dozens of times before, right down to the chair I sat in.

But this time was different.

A few hours after I got home, a rash broke out on my neck and scalp. At first, I didn't think anything of it. But as the itching and redness increased, I realized I was having some sort of allergic reaction. I went to a local drugstore and picked up a topical cream meant to soothe inflamed skin. Imagine my surprise when the condition didn't respond to any over-the-counter products. In fact, it got worse. It spread to my arms, legs, chest, and back. Now I started to worry. As a doctor, I try to consider my own health concerns clinically. However, even from a medical perspective, the rash and inflammation were getting worse remarkably fast. Soon my skin felt like it was on fire. I could barely sleep in my own bed because the cotton sheets chafed like sandpaper.

I made an appointment with a friend from medical school who had become chair of the dermatology department at George Washington University. She confirmed that the hair-coloring chemical *paraphenylenediamine* (PPD) had caused my condition. When PPD is processed into hair dye, it can cause allergic reactions over time and with repeated exposure. The reactions range from mild to severe, and I was at the wrong end of that spectrum. Following standard protocol, she prescribed long-term topical steroids. She also added a six-month ban on coloring my hair. As if the ban was not hard enough, you can imagine my concern when the rash and pain just got worse.

Next, I consulted a renowned allergist who had treated several US presidents. He ran skin-patch tests and did some research of his own, but the best he could do was confirm that I was allergic to hair products with PPD. I also reacted to other common but hard-to-pronounce ingredients in skin creams and beauty products. Adding to the frustration, I became hypersensitive to the UV rays in sunlight. He prescribed powerful antihistamine medications, topical antibiotics, and oral steroids. As a doctor, I knew all too well that antibiotics, steroids, and prescription antihistamines often do more harm than good. They create a toxic imbalance in the body. Personally, I prefer, whenever possible, to use fewer drugs, not more. I'm a proponent of turning to nature for solutions when it is medically appropriate. It just didn't seem like there was any apparent alternative to all the things that these doctors had prescribed for me. As an unfortunate bonus, the allergist extended the ban on hair coloring to the rest of my life.

Finally, I approached a renowned infectious disease specialist at Medstar Washington Hospital Center. The news got worse. He suggested that I might have a systemic bacterial infection. That caused him to pull out a prescription pad to give me a powerful antibiotic only recently approved by the FDA. He also recommended soaking in a tub full of diluted bleach two to three times a week. You can probably relate to how I felt about that!

There I was, having highly accomplished skincare experts throwing dangerous chemicals and drugs at me. The problem is, the more powerful the drug, the more devastating the potential side effects. The steroids alone can cause weight gain, mood swings, and increase the risk of infections and other serious conditions. Powerful prescription antibiotics kill good bacteria just as quickly as bad. They can throw your entire gastrointestinal system out of whack.

It was no wonder that I became increasingly anxious, which only made my skin condition more severe. The more stressed I became, the worse it got and the more exhausted and ragged I looked. I needed a solution. Despite consultations with all these talented doctors, all I had was a vague diagnosis: "multiple chemical hyper-sensitivity." That and the same old discomfort and suffering. As a doctor who had avoided prescription drugs for most of my life, I was distressed to be on a cocktail of them.

I decided to attack the problem from the other side—eliminating the potential cause of my skin problems. I tossed out almost everything in my bathroom. No perfumes, no dyes, no chemical additives. I bought special chemical-free soap to bathe and wash my clothes and bed linens. I couldn't wear makeup or beauty products. I even tossed out my mattress and replaced it with a nontoxic, certified organic model. Coloring my hair now meant spending the better part of a day at a specialty salon that used henna made in-house. It's amazing how difficult it can be to live without the convenience of all the synthetics and chemicals that permeate our lives.

I slowly got better. But my skin was peppered with scars and lesions from the constant scratching and trauma. Even worse, my hair was falling out. Tired of taking so many medications, I started researching homeopathic solutions. But I couldn't find anything that showed promise to completely resolve the issue.

Around the same time, my husband was being treated for chronic and severe Crohn's disease. He had battled the miserable illness for ten years, suffering from abdominal pain, loose stools, and fatigue. But his condition had recently worsened. His gastroenterologist was aggressively pushing him to go on a long-term course of biologics —powerful drugs made from the DNA of microbes. It would have required regular, painful injections, potentially for years. The treatment includes risks of infections, cancer, and other life-threatening side effects. It was a classic case of the treatment being just marginally better than the disease itself.

I was firmly against using biologics. My husband had recently left his career in the incredibly high-stress world of hedge fund trading, and we were slowly but surely making positive life changes to lessen his stress and live healthier. Biologics didn't fit that philosophy. We started looking for nontoxic solutions and decided to experiment with CBD, a cannabinoid found in both marijuana and hemp. I had heard of CBD but didn't have any firsthand experience with it.

CBD is derived from marijuana and hemp plants, but it isn't the intoxicating component of the plants. The stuff that gets people high—and can be used for medically necessary pain treatment and other uses—is a compound called tetrahydrocannabinol, better known as THC. Both plants have the CBD and THC compounds. But hemp-derived CBD contains less than 0.3 percent of THC. That's way too little to experience any intoxicating effects.

My husband started using CBD. To my surprise and his delight, daily pure CBD oil improved his Crohn's symptoms dramatically. He got so much better, he was able to reduce his medications and avoid the toxic biologics. He still suffers from Crohn's, but it's much easier to tolerate because of the CBD. The relief changed his life!

Intrigued, I thought that CBD might offer relief for my skin condition. One of my husband's friends owns and operates a high-end beauty product development laboratory with a reputation for using premium, pure, nontoxic ingredients. We met with him and discussed creating a skin serum with extremely pure CBD. We went back and forth, trying out one formula after another. It was a laborious process of trial-and-error, and we were lucky to have him helping us. He was as patient as he was skilled in the chemistry of formulating beauty products. I enlisted nurses I worked with to act as test subjects, and they absolutely loved what we came up with. But we continued to refine the formula. Because of my sensitivity, we couldn't use typical beauty product ingredients such as petrolatum, phthalates, sulfates, formaldehyde, or even artificial dyes. Finally, after a lot of experimentation, research, and going down blind alleys, we settled on a serum I could try.

We all felt a good deal of excitement the first time I tried it. I also braced myself because I didn't want to get my hopes up. I applied the serum to select parts of my neck and scalp, on my ears and chest, and around my hairline—"patch testing" to make sure I didn't have a negative reaction. Out of curiosity, I also put some on my face. Right away, I felt relieved of the need to scratch, which I had been doing every day nearly constantly, causing my rash to get more and more irritated. As I felt relief, I weaned myself off the antihistamines I had been taking, which always made me sleepy and in need of a cup of coffee.

I could hardly believe it. Not only did the CBD serum lessen my pain and itching, it slowly eliminated the remaining rash and skin lesions. I also noticed that the puffiness under my eyes went away, and my skin tone and appearance became clearer. The best part: I did not experience any side effects. We were so excited and happy with the formula we had created that we decided to produce it for consumers under a company we named Aethera. Aethera is derived from the idea of the classical element of *ether* and the oscillation of sunlight. Our goal was to create an idea of something ethereal that, like pure beauty, was truly elusive. Even if perceptible, it couldn't really be captured or subjugated.

It was such a relief to see the skin problems go away. But it also came with a wonderful and unexpected additional benefit. My skin looked amazing! My skin was brighter, had more even tones, and my fine lines appeared smoother. Close friends and colleagues started commenting on my appearance. Some said I looked youthful, which felt so good! Friends demanded the name of the dermatologist I was using or wanted me to reveal the treatments I was having. ("C'mon, it's dermabrasion, right? No? Chemical peel?") The nurses at work asked if I had started a new workout regimen.

My skin was radiant and glowed with good health. That's not something you'll get from the steroids or superstrong antibiotics they tried to give me for my skin condition. That led me to start researching the antiaging properties of CBD, and what I found was, frankly, stunning. All the available studies I read backed up my own experience and then some.

In 2018, a piece of federal legislation known as the 2018 Farm Act legalized hemp, which has led to an explosion of research into CBD and other cannabinoids.[1] It will certainly take a while for the medical community to exploit all the potential in medical cannabis, but there is absolutely no debate about that potential.

My experience made me wonder: If CBD is a scientifically valid approach for many medical conditions, then how come everyone doesn't know about it? How come everyone with a skin condition—or anyone who wanted his or her skin to look noticeably younger and healthier—wasn't using CBD and perhaps other cannabinoids on a regular basis? The answer is found, at least partially, in the history of cannabis and CBD in the United States.

---

1. Hemp Farming Act of 2018. H.R.5485, 115th Cong., 2nd sess., *Congressional Record* 165 (April 12, 2018), HR 5485. https://www.congress.gov/bill/115th-congress/house-bill/5485.

2 · CBD THROUGH THE AGES

THE PLANT SPECIES THAT contains both hemp and marijuana is called *Cannabis sativa*. It has an extensive history because it's been cultivated for thousands of years by cultures and civilizations around the world. In the right climate, cannabis is easy to grow, and it is fairly simple to harvest for its beneficial compounds. The majority of ancient peoples considered the plant wholly beneficial. The demonizing of cannabis is actually a relatively modern trend.

Hemp and marijuana are the two main varieties of *Cannabis sativa*. Their cultivation can be traced back possibly more than ten thousand years to the Neolithic period, when crops were first domesticated. Archaeologists have discovered hemp rope fragments from this period.[2] It was also used throughout the early Asian empire for textiles and other common materials—just as it would be going forward. Hemp was eventually used to mass-produce paper, which opened the door to the rise of literature in ancient China.[3]

There's evidence that the Chinese tapped into the medicinal potential of the plant by making hempseeds and oil part of their diet. Oil made from hempseed and other parts of the plant is rich in fatty and amino acids. No wonder, then, that it has been used in consumable preparations such as salad oil and as a component in topical applications for healthy and beautiful skin and hair. Hemp oil has also been used historically as a drying agent in paints and varnishes.[4]

The Chinese also realized the medical potential of the psychoactive strains of *Cannabis sativa*—those containing *tetrahydrocannabinol*—which are better known as THC. They used THC for teas that worked as painkillers, to treat

---

2. Ernest L. Abel, *Marihuana: The First Twelve Thousand Years* (New York: Plenum Press, 1943; repr., NY: Springer Science + Business Media, 1980), 4.

3. Mark Cartwright, "Paper in Ancient China," Ancient History Encyclopedia, September 15, 2017, https://www.ancient.eu/article/1120/paper-in-ancient-china/.

4. Robert C. Clarke and Mark D. Merlin, *Cannabis: Evolution and Ethnobotany* (Berkeley, CA: University of California Press; rep. 2013), 208.

gout, and to treat mental conditions. About five thousand years ago, a Chinese emperor commonly known as Shen Nung, who many consider the "Father of Chinese Medicine," advocated for medical marijuana in perhaps the first pharmaceutical reference work, *Pén-tsʾao Ching*.[5] Archaeologists believe ancient Chinese surgeons mixed THC with wine to make a simple surgical anesthesia.[6]

When the plant made its way to my native India, its psychoactive properties were integrated into spiritual, non-medicinal practice. Some of the earliest written references to the plant are included in the sacred Hindu texts, the *Vedas*, which mention cannabis as one of five sacred plants.[7] In fact, *bhang* is a traditional Indian beverage made with milk sweeteners, other flavorings, and marijuana paste.[8] The beverage is sold in India to this day. Creating a slight, relaxing high, the drink became, and remains, a mainstay element in Hindu cultural and spiritual practices. It is even sold at government-certified shops.

---

5. Eileen Konieczny and Lauren Wilson, *Healing With CBD: How Cannabidiol Can Transform Your Health Without the High* (Berkeley, CA: Ulysses Press, 2018), 19; David E. Newton, *Marijuana: A Reference Handbook*, 2nd ed. (Santa Barbara, CA: ABC-CLIO, 2017), 15

6. Newton, *Marijuana: A Reference Handbook*, 2nd ed., 15.

7. Newton, *Marijuana: A Reference Handbook*, 2nd ed., 17.

8. Newton, *Marijuana: A Reference Handbook*, 2nd ed., 17.

Indians also incorporated cannabis into treatments for a range of medical conditions as part of Ayurvedic medicine. Indian herbalists prescribed cannabis preparations for headaches, gastrointestinal disorders, and many other maladies. This was part of the traditional Indian holistic approach to well-being, a practice that adopted plants into a health regimen. I was exposed to this way of thinking about health from a very young age and was aware of Ayurvedic medicine even before my years of medical training. So my Indian heritage has probably made me more open to the healing properties of cannabis than more conventional doctors might be.

Eventually, cannabis found its way to the Middle East, where Persian doctors appreciated its ability to reduce people's pain. Other cultures in the region shared an appreciation for the plant and its uses. However, Muslim officials enacted what may have been the very first prohibition, regulating against the use of psychoactive cannabis because many felt it was an intoxicant explicitly forbidden by the Quran.[9]

Cannabis sativa enjoyed a receptive audience in ancient Greece and Rome. Both took advantage of the medical applications of marijuana and the practical uses of hemp. Hemp was an everyday plant and textile in ancient

---

9. Newton, *Marijuana: A Reference Handbook*, 2nd ed., 53.

Greece.[10] The ancient Greeks used the plant to treat human ailments such as tapeworms, earaches, and inflammation, and they also pioneered its use in veterinary medicine. Their philosophers and medical professionals wrote extensively about the plant's potential. Romans embraced it as well. Claudius Galen, one of ancient Rome's most notable physicians, espoused its medicinal value.[11] Roman farmers turned the crop into thread for rope and grain sacks.

An entire book could be written about the history of hemp, and that's not my goal, so I'll skim a bit. The Middle Ages could be called hemp's golden age. In the colder climates, places such as Germany, Russia, and even Britain, the weather lent itself to hemp cultivation but less so to growing marijuana. There is even evidence that the Vikings grew hemp. Hemp was a mainstay crop throughout medieval and Renaissance Europe and Britain. It was used extensively to make strong rope and sails.

The Britain of King James grew massive hemp crops for its textile trade. Historical traces of the plant and hemp products can be found in modern England, Scotland, Wales, and Ireland.[12] Because one of the primary uses of hemp textiles was in ropes and sails, the plant largely

---

10. Clarke and Merlin, *Cannabis: Evolution and Ethnobotany*, 160.

11. Martin Booth, *Cannabis: A History* (New York: Thomas Dunne Books, 2004), 31.

12. Newton, *Marijuana: A Reference Handbook*, 2nd ed., 25.

equipped the growing British naval fleet (and it was even used to make some naval uniforms), giving hemp a key role in British imperial expansion. Consequently, French and British colonies in North America adopted the plant as part of the imported culture and industry.

Hemp was widely grown in colonial America because authorities directed all farmers to set aside a prescribed portion of their acreage for the cultivation of the crop, as it was considered crucial to the success of the new outposts. Although there was a native strain of cannabis growing wild in America (known commonly as "Indian Hemp"), colonial farmers generally grew the domesticated *Cannabis sativa* brought as seed from Britain. The crops were tenacious; the fibers from the plant were long and had incredible strength, and hemp was easy to grow. It did not deplete soil nutrients as tobacco did and could be grown perpetually on the same plot of land. Eventually, luminaries of independence, including Thomas Jefferson and George Washington, would add it to the crops they grew on their own plantations. An "acre of the best ground" was reserved for hemp on Jefferson's Poplar Forest plantation.[13] Locally grown hemp would eventually become essential thanks to the need to replace British

---

13. Ben Swenson, "Hemp & Flax in Colonial America," *The Colonial Williamsburg Journal* (Winter 2015), https://www.history.org/Foundation/journal/Winter15/hemp.cfm.

imports as hostilities between the colonies and the home country increased.

Marijuana played a lesser role in colonial life. The early Americans almost certainly knew that the plant could be consumed—and given that tobacco was grown along with cannabis, it's natural that some colonists would have attempted to smoke it. But practical applications were more pressing, and hemp was used for weaving clothing, bed linens, cord and rope, and other "industrial" uses. The plant remained widespread in the colonies and in early America as the new nation expanded westward.

But as the country grew and matured, more lucrative cash crops that were easier to process, such as cotton, replaced hemp in textiles. Marijuana became the more common plant for general use. It saw fairly widespread application in the late 1800s as major medical companies created tinctures and formulas incorporating cannabis, marketing the products for use as painkillers, anti-spasmodics, anti-nausea, and more.[14] Some of these products competed directly with more powerful opiate-based medications.

That's where cannabis got caught up in the proliferation of opium abuse and repercussions from Prohibition in the early part of the twentieth century. The most significant impact on the cultivation and use of hemp and marijuana was perhaps the Marihuana Tax Act of 1937.

14. Konieczny and Wilson, *Healing With CBD*, 24–25.

The act outlawed all types of *Cannabis sativa* and products made with them.[15] The drug was effectively forced underground, and a black market was created that supplied demand.

This was, in part, a reaction to the cultural stereotypes captured in *Reefer Madness,* a movie released in 1936. It fascinated and horrified the public with its propagandist vilification of marijuana as a psychosis-inducing drug destroying the nation. The blatant falsehoods depicted by the movie would set the tone for political and cultural biases against anything cannabis, prejudice that persists to this day.

Smoking marijuana became associated with "undesirables" like blues musicians, brown-skinned immigrants, and low-income communities of color. The 1938 Pure Food, Drug, and Cosmetics Act laid the foundation for future restrictions on narcotics of all types. By the time America entered World War II, marijuana was banned in every state. In addition, the use of hemp in any industrial capacity had virtually ceased by the 1940s, and future uses were curtailed by the explosion of plastics in the war and postwar industrial boom. The final nail in the coffin of both recreational and medicinal marijuana (and hemp) was the 1951 Boggs Act, which established severe man-

15. Newton, *Marijuana: A Reference Handbook*, 2nd ed., 65–66.

datory prison sentences and high fines for possession of even a small amount of marijuana.[16]

The various laws would not stop the Beat Generation from heartily embracing marijuana use during the late 1950s and 1960s.[17]

Richard Nixon pioneered the "war on drugs," which lumped marijuana in with far more dangerous narcotics like heroin. In 1970, marijuana was officially classified as a Schedule 1 drug, joining LSD and heroin in a group that the government deemed to have a significant potential for abuse and "no currently accepted medical use."[18] The repeated efforts to reclassify recreational and medical marijuana have failed. Marijuana continues to be treated like a street drug at the federal level. Unfortunately, the classification is overly broad, and—until very recently—it included hemp and non-intoxicating components such as CBD. In the United States, these legislative assaults essentially killed any research into the medicinal value of not only marijuana and its psychoactive components, but also the more benign compounds found in hemp.

However, that's changing. Late in the twentieth century, many states pushed back against the illogical federal

---

16. Newton, *Marijuana: A Reference Handbook*, 2nd ed., 66.

17. Konieczny and Wilson, *Healing With CBD*, 30–31.

18. "Drug Scheduling," United States Drug Enforcement Administration, n.d., https://www.dea.gov/drug-scheduling.

ban. In fact, less than three years after marijuana was listed as a Schedule 1 narcotic, Oregon became the first state to decriminalize it.[19] The decriminalization trend continued throughout the 1970s and 1980s. In 1996, California became the first state in the country to legalize medical marijuana.[20] In the decade that followed, more than half the states in the country voted to permit medical marijuana.

Then, in 2012, California and Washington became the first states to fully legalize all forms of cannabis. That opened the floodgates and, state by state, the legalization movement has gained steam. But for skincare product consumers, the more important development has been the 2018 Farm Bill, which legalized the growing of hemp nationally. That allowed for the use of hemp-derived CBD in products across the country and led to a rush of products hitting the market that contain this cannabinoid. The law allows for the sale federally of CBD products containing less than 0.3 percent THC. However, some states and localities have enacted legislation essentially outlawing CBD—which is why you should check your local and state laws before purchasing CBD products through the mail or online.

---

19. Newton, *Marijuana: A Reference Handbook*, 2nd ed., 112–113.

20. Mark Bourrie, *Hemp: A Short History of the Most Misunderstood Plant and Its Uses and Abuses* (Buffalo, NY: Firefly Books, 2003), 98.

Legalizing cannabis means it can be funded for research. It also creates a business opportunity, which drives innovation. That means exciting new discoveries are coming to light as scientists study what was once stigmatized and forbidden.

That has been both good and bad news. On the positive side, a vast number of consumers now have access to a wide range of CBD skincare and well-being products. The last few years have seen an explosion of CBD-infused skincare offerings—from face masks to skin lotions, bath beads, and more.

But no legislation can plan for all eventualities. Some product claims made by manufacturers have been overblown or outright false. Independent testing has found that some products claiming to be CBD-based contain little or no CBD. The quality of the CBD oil used in some products is also an open question, one that cannot be answered by current labeling regulations. It is not just that a few manufacturers are playing fast and loose with the law, it is that consumer laws pertaining to CBD use in products are poorly defined or non-existent. Regulation has not caught up with reality.

Complicating all this are historical trends and cultural prejudices, which take a long time to reverse. The twentieth-century vilification of *Cannabis sativa* in all its many forms lingers in many states and especially at the federal level. There is, as I write this, still a great deal of confusion about where even CBD products are legal. It would make sense that CBD from hemp should now be legal and available nationwide thanks to the 2018 Farm Bill. But not everyone operates on good sense.

In addition, research on the benefits and efficacy of CBD in relation to specific diseases and conditions (including in topical formulations, as well as ingestible forms), is ongoing. That experimentation is in its preliminary stages and there is a long way to go. We are only just starting to learn how CBD functions within the different layers of skin and with different skin cells. Not all manufacturers are formulating products with the latest study results in mind. This is an exciting time but also a confusing one. The medical potential for CBD and other cannabinoids is undeniable, but medical research takes time and careful analysis. Commercial uses tend to speed ahead of research.

The medical landscape today presents a bit of a challenge for skincare patients looking to enlist medical providers well-versed in the latest research and data about medical marijuana, CBD, and other cannabinoids. The place to start in your search for a healthcare partner is with your state's medical board. Many are establishing certification programs for doctors and other professionals such as nurse practitioners. I completed the certification program in Maryland and DC and am continuing my education and training to stay current with the latest research and medical updates. Even if your state does not have certification requirements or training, many medical providers are taking it upon themselves (as I have) to train and become certified through third-party organizations.

The current moment presents unprecedented opportunities for CBD as it shakes off the stigma of recent history and scientists and doctors integrate it into their practice. The future is promising for CBD and skincare, and it will reward the well-informed consumer.

3 · HOW CBD WORKS

UNDERSTANDING THE SKINCARE POTENTIAL of CBD starts with understanding what it is and what it is not. CBD is low risk and will not get anyone "high." It does not have the intoxicating effects of its cousin, THC.

CBD and THC are related because they are oils derived from the same flowering plant family, Cannabaceae. Within the genus *Cannabis*, there are three species: *Cannabis sativa*, *Cannabis indica*, and *Cannabis ruderalis*. It is important to know that the term "cannabis" is not interchangeable with "marijuana." Marijuana was coined in the twentieth century as any cannabis variety traditionally cultivated for its intoxicating properties, typically averaging 5 to 30 percent THC content. Hemp is specifically *Cannabis sativa* that contains no more than 0.3 percent

THC. As discussed in Chapter 2, hemp has historically been grown for industrial use and medical purposes. There are now efforts to abolish the designation "marijuana," because its origins were founded on racist associations with Mexican workers becoming high with specific strains of cannabis. For ease of differentiation, I will continue to use the term marijuana at this time.

Hemp is generally a better source for CBD because of the plant's high concentration of the compound and the fact that hemp CBD can be isolated largely free of the much more controversial THC. As interests surge for low-cost and high-volume production of pure CBD uncontaminated by THC, scientists in both the US and Canada have genetically modified yeast to produce isolates of CBD and isolates of THC. Researchers at the University of Kentucky, in partnership with GenCanna, have cultivated a chemotype of hemp that is 100 percent free of THC.[21] It is an important distinction because so many people have hang-ups about marijuana and its intoxicating effects.

---

21. Tom Latek, "Hemp Manufacturer GenCanna Teams with UK Researchers, Says They Have a Material with Zero THC," *Northern Kentucky Tribune*, Kentucky Center for Public Service Journalism, January 30, 2019, https://www.nkytribune.com/2019/01/hemp -manufacturer-gencanna-teams-with-uk-researchers-says-they -have-a-material-with-zero-thc/.

The therapeutic power inherent in cannabis plants—including hemp—is largely contained in the group of compounds we know as *cannabinoids*. Researchers have identified more than one hundred cannabinoids, and it's likely that new ones will be discovered in the future.[22] CBD is just one of these compounds.

There is a fascinating parallel with the way the plants and our bodies are wired. All of these cannabinoids interact with the *phytocannabinoid* system (phyto means plant), which regulates the growth and functions of the cannabis plant. That system has a twin in the human body's *endocannabinoid* system (ECS), a network of receptors, neurotransmitters, and enzymes that interact to maintain healthy balance in the body. That's why grasping the mechanisms by which CBD works in your body starts with understanding its plant source.

Cannabis contains medically significant amounts of only a handful of these beneficial compounds. The standouts include CBD, CBN, CBC, CBG, and THC. Most other cannabinoids can be considered complementary and incidental to these. THC is, of course, the one that gets the most public scrutiny and scientific interest

22. Genevieve Lafaye, et al., "Cannabis, Cannabinoids, and Health," *Dialogues in Clinical Neuroscience* 19, no. 3 (September 2017): 309–16, https://www.ncbi.nlm.nih.gov/pmc/articles /PMC5741114/.

because it is a psychoactive intoxicant. As I chronicled in Chapter 2, THC's effect on users is why it has been so widely vilified in society and by the American government. That has long clouded the fact that THC has a great number of potentially important therapeutic applications. But as truly powerful and full of medical potential as THC is, the most common cannabinoid in all forms of the cannabis plant is CBD.[23]

The Endocannabinoid System

CBD works through the endocannabinoid system (ECS), the network that maintains healthy balance in the body. "Endo" is a prefix for *endogenous*, which describes anything produced inside the body. So, as the name implies, the system regulates cannabinoids that your body produces. But this is the great thing—the system also responds to externally introduced cannabinoids, such as the compounds from the cannabis plant.

In fact, fish and animals small and large all have internal endocannabinoid systems that match up perfectly with cannabis's phytocannabinoid system. This compatibility between plant and animal systems accounts for the safety of CBD and other cannabinoids—including THC.

---

23. Leonard Leinow and Juliana Birnbaum, *CBD: A Patient's Guide to Medicinal Cannabis* (Berkeley, CA: North Atlantic Books, 2017), xxii.

In cases where resistance builds up or a user experiences a reaction, it's best to discontinue use and seek the advice of a medical professional. But, as with all things cannabis, we continue to learn about the ECS, and research will surely teach us even more in the years to come. In fact, we have only even known about the existence of the ECS for about twenty-five years; it was first described in the 1990s.[24]

However, we can boil it down somewhat. The goal of the ECS is to ensure well-being by keeping your body in healthy balance—a state known as *homeostasis*. In particular, the system seeks to return the body to "normal" in the face of ever-changing external factors, such as temperature variations or allergens. The ECS modulates pleasure and other psychophysical sensations and makes corrections whenever the body's health is threatened by injury or disease.

The system plays an important part in an impressive range of functions such as immune system efficiency, sleep-wake cycles, perceptions of hot, cold, and pain, general mood, digestive system function, cell death and regeneration, memory issues, and more.

---

24. Michael H. Moskowitz, *Medical Cannabis: A Guide for Patients, Practitioners, and Caregivers* (Virginia Beach, VA: Köehler Books, 2017), 14–15.

ECS receptors are essential to the function of the system. They are often described as "locks" that cannabinoids fit as a "key." Two crucial ECS receptors have been identified. They are known as CB1 and CB2 (more are likely to be discovered in the future).

CB1 receptors are abundant in the central nervous system, especially in the brain. CB2 receptors are more plentiful in "periphery" tissue such as organs. As our largest organ, the skin (averaging 8 pounds and 22 square feet in adults) contains a wealth of both types. The skin is a huge sensor jammed full of receptors that enable the fast-moving brain to keep in touch with what is going on in the outside world. The receptors are turned on or off by "signaling" molecules.

The two prominent endogenous, or internally produced, "signaling" molecules that work on those receptors are *anandamide* (AEA) and 2-arachidonoylglycerol (2-AG)—a receptor "agonist" that is more common in the brain. (Agonists are molecules that bind to receptors.) There are five identified enzymes in the system that synthesize or break down (as the situation calls for it) those two signaling molecules.[25] That may sound a little complicated, but it's actually a fairly basic process of action and reaction that lies at the heart of how CBD affects your ECS, in contrast to how THC impacts the system.

---

25. Leinow and Birnbaum, *CBD: A Patient's Guide*, 16.

THC binds to CB1 receptors. CBD, on the other hand, does not technically bind to either the CB1 or CB2 receptors. Instead, CBD influences how other compounds—most importantly enzymes—impact the ECS. For instance, a particular enzyme, FAAH, breaks down and removes anandamide from your system. Anandamide is known as the "bliss" molecule and is in fact named for the Sanskrit *ananda*, meaning "joy" or "bliss." Anandamide is an incredibly important signaling molecule. It binds to both CB1 and CB2 receptors. As the name implies, it contributes to a general feeling of well-being and can combat debilitating mental conditions such as anxiety and depression. Anandamide also plays a role in appetite, pain relief, and even sexuality and reproduction. You want more of it, not less. Under stress, FAAH increasingly suppresses and breaks down anandamide, stimulating fear, anxiety, and pain. CBD suppresses FAAH. This in turn allows for an increase in anandamide. So, while CBD might not bind to the receptors itself, it has just as powerful an effect as if it did. CBD has far less interaction with anandamide's cousin, 2-AG.

It's important to note that although these two receptor agonists are the best known and researched at this point, they are not alone. But we know far less about the others, and it will be some time before research unlocks their secrets. Still, it's worth keeping abreast of developments.

CB1 and CB2 sometimes act in opposition to maintain health equilibrium. For instance, activation of CB1 receptors in response to trauma can increase lipid levels, while CB2 receptors may be triggered at the same time to reduce liver inflammation and resulting lipid levels.[26] Ultimately, the point is that the ECS is continually trying to help the body maintain homeostasis.

All this makes the ECS sound like it's a mechanical system, the same person to person. However, that's not true. The ECS in your body is unique to you; consequently, so are the reactions you'll experience to different dosages of CBD and THC. It's vitally important to understand the need to monitor your body closely whenever you use any cannabinoid, even if you're following general recommendations like the ones in this book. Also keep in mind that the science surrounding the ECS, CBD, and other cannabinoids is still relatively young and fast evolving. Most relevant studies have taken place within the last two decades—a blink of the eye in terms of scientific inquiry. More discoveries are sure to be made in the coming years as research into plant-based cannabinoids increases behind legislative changes. I urge you to keep abreast of new developments by checking in with one or

---

26. Moskowitz, *Medical Cannabis: A Guide for Patients, Practitioners, and Caregivers*, 25–26.

more of the general reference sources in the Resources section at the end of this book.

Potential Benefits of CBD

I want to make it clear that even though I'm a strong advocate of CBD and other cannabinoids as potentially significant medical tools, I don't believe that any of these is a cure-all. Unfortunately, whenever a new potential treatment with a lot of promise comes along, there are inevitably a lot of claims made before research establishes the reality. You can easily find anecdotal stories online about people curing serious diseases ranging from migraines to multiple sclerosis using CBD oil.

The most famous of these is Rick Simpson's story of curing his own basal cell carcinoma—skin cancer on his face and neck—with high-THC oil alone. According to his much-publicized story, he cured himself in a matter of days with topical applications of high-dose THC oil. Simpson advocates for a process of extracting THC and other cannabinoids from the plant using solvents, which I don't consider a good idea for a number of reasons. The method and resulting oil is called RSO. In any case, even if Simpson's case is absolutely true—and I don't have any reason to doubt him—it's incredibly important to keep in mind that one case is not a representative sample. The science and available research strongly indicate that CBD, especially in conjunction with THC, has powerful potential cancer-prevention and cancer-fighting properties.[27] But I would not recommend to a patient that they turn to cannabinoids alone to cure cancer. I believe a balanced approach is always a good idea, and you need to use your judgment when choosing what traditional and unconventional methods and substances you'll use to treat your own disorders or conditions.

The point is, I consider CBD an excellent complement to traditional medical treatments. I think it offers incredible potential as a treatment for skincare and myriad other health concerns. Yes, sometimes a CBD-heavy formulation or supplement alone may clear up a skin condition or help you sleep better. But for more serious health issues, it's good to consider all potential treatments and consult with your physician before beginning an informed and balanced treatment plan.

That said, the wide range of CBD's potentially beneficial properties is astounding. This much is absolutely clear and has been established: CBD has a profound effect

---

27. Barbara Dariš, et al., "Cannabinoids in Cancer Treatment: Therapeutic Potential and Legislation," *The Bosnian Journal of Basic Medical Sciences* 19, no. 1 (February 2019), 14–23, https://doi.org/10.17305/bjbms.2018.3532; Paweł Śledziński, et al., "The Current State and Future Perspectives of Cannabinoids in Cancer Biology," *Cancer Medicine* 7, no. 3 (March 2018): 765–75, https://doi.org/10.1002/cam4.1312.

on your ECS, and your ECS has a profound effect on all aspects of your physical, mental, and skin health.

Where your skin is concerned, CBD offers some really interesting benefits. It spurs collagen development, helping skin stay plump and youthful. In fact, one of the areas in which CBD shows the most promise is slowing the effects of aging (what is generally called "photoaging" in skincare because the sun's UV rays are the main culprit in premature skin aging). That topic is covered in depth in Chapter 7, but that one quality goes far in explaining the explosion of CBD-infused beauty products currently hitting the retail market.

Regardless of what you might choose to use it for, the key reason CBD creates so much excitement in doctors and researchers is that, unlike many new drugs and treatments, the risk of side effects with CBD is minimal.[28] In fact, studies have found it can be useful for treating opiate

28. Mateus Machado Bergamaschi, et al., "Safety and Side Effects of Cannabidiol, a *Cannabis sativa* Constituent," *Current Drug Safety* 6, no. 4 (September 2011): 237–49, https://doi.org/10.2174/157488611798280924.

addiction in chronic pain sufferers.[29] At its June 2018 meeting, the World Health Organization Expert Committee on Drug Dependence (ECDD) concluded that, in its pure state, cannabidiol does not have abuse or dependency potential or cause any public-health-related harm.[30] In many instances, CBD used in conjunction with medical THC will moderate the intoxicating effects of the psychoactive cannabinoid.

29. Yann Chye, et al., "The Endocannabinoid System and Cannabidiol's Promise for the Treatment of Substance Use Disorder," *Frontiers in Psychiatry* 10, no. 63 (February 2019): n.p., https://www.frontiersin.org/articles/10.3389/fpsyt.2019.00063/full; Amanda Reiman, Mark Welty, and Perry Solomon, "Cannabis as a Substitute for Opioid-Based Pain Medication: Patient Self-Report," *Cannabis and Cannabinoid Research* 2, no. 1 (June 2017): 160–66, https://doi.org/10.1089/can.2017.0012; Kevin F. Boehnke, Evangelos Litinas, and Daniel J. Clauw, "Medical Cannabis Use is Associated with Decreased Opiate Medication Use in a Retrospective Cross-Sectional Survey of Patients with Chronic Pain," *The Journal of Pain* 17, no. 6 (June 2016): 739–44, https://doi.org/10.1016/j.jpain.2016.03.002; Gustavo Gonzalez-Cuevas, et al., "Unique Treatment Potential of Cannabidiol for the Prevention of Relapse to Drug Use: Preclinical Proof of Principle," *Neuropsychopharmacology* 43, no. 10 (September 2018): 2036–45, https://doi.org/10.1038/s41386-018-0050-8.

30. World Health Organization. *WHO Expert Committee on Drug Dependence, Fortieth Report.* WHO Technical Report Series No. 1013 (Geneva, Switzerland: World Health Organization, 2018): 13–16, https://apps.who.int/iris/bitstream/handle/10665/279948/9789241210225-eng.pdf?ua=1.

4 · THE ENTOURAGE EFFECT

CANNABINOIDS IN ISOLATION—like CBD oil—can have a significant health benefit. But when grouped together, they amplify each other's beneficial effects through what's called the *entourage effect*. The most common combination is CBD with THC. For instance, to control seizures in children, medical professionals have successfully used a CBD to THC ratio of 18:1 or 20:1. A ratio of 1:1 is common for pain control or 2:1 to aid in sleep. But CBD also shows great potential as a partner to lesser-known cannabinoids, including the following:

- THCA. This is the acidic and non-psychoactive precursor of THC (it becomes THC via light exposure, heat, or natural drying or aging of the plant).

THCA (tetrahydrocannabinolic acid) can be consumed by juicing or eating the raw leaves of the cannabis plant. This cannabinoid shows promise as a treatment for epilepsy, some forms of pain, arthritis, and nausea.

- CBDA. As with THCA, CBDA (cannabidiolic acid) is an acidic cannabinoid that is also non-psychoactive and a precursor of CBD. It converts to CBD through the same processes as THCA does to THC. CBDA combats nausea and has most of the curative properties of CBD. It can be consumed by eating raw parts of the plant, or those parts can be distilled with alcohol to make tinctures or other formulas. I believe CBDA holds a great deal of potential. It is an area of scientific inquiry that has been on the back burner due to the popularity of CBD.

- CBGA. Cannabigerolic acid is the precursor to THCA and CBDA and is also non-psychoactive. Unheated, CBGA is being studied for roles in reducing inflammation and pain, promoting bone growth, and treating schizophrenia and some cancers.

- CBG. Cannabigerol is present only in low amounts in cannabis. It is being studied as a strong glaucoma treatment, but nothing is conclusive yet. It may also have potential as an antibacterial and as general protection against neurological damage.

- CBCA. Cannabichromenic acid is used to treat fungal infections such as ringworm and athlete's foot.

- CBC. A supporting cannabinoid that doesn't directly affect CB1 or CB2 receptors, CBC (cannabichromene) boosts other cannabinoids, indirectly helping with mood disorders and possibly playing a role in fighting certain cancers.

- CBN. CBN (cannabinol) shows a great deal of promise. It is derived from THCA. It's part of a bevy of cannabinoids being used in skincare. Its benefits include pain relief, fighting bacteria, reducing inflammation, and appetite stimulation.

- THCV. A lesser-known cousin to THC, THCV (tetrahydrocannabivarin) shows potential to reduce convulsions and work as an appetite suppressant.

- CBDV. Essentially a less powerful version of CBD, cannabidivarin plays a part in reducing seizures and fighting nausea.

Of all these, the most common combination involves some ratio of CBD to THC. The sum is more than the parts because the two cannabinoids bind to different receptors. They have similar properties—relief of pain and itching, antioxidant, etc.—which means they provide a two-pronged attack against pain, inflammation, itching, and other symptoms. This is part of what some professionals call "whole plant medicine."

The problem is that although CBD products can theoretically be sold nationwide (some states and localities outlaw the purchase of CBD), THC can only be sold in states where it is legal for at least medicinal purposes. Other cannabinoids may or may not be available in isolation for the same reason. But let's be clear here: combining CBD and THC topically does not mean you'll get high. For instance, if you rub on a lotion containing both CBD and THC, you won't experience any psychoactive effects. Depending on the type of oil or cream and other ingredients in the formula, the lotion may not contain any components that can pass through the skin's barrier, let alone pass through the blood-brain barrier. If the formula can't get by those barriers, the THC only impacts the layers of the skin and won't make you high. In fact, in the lab for our cosmetics company, we are exploring using THC to boost the effectiveness of the CBD. However, there is a complex web of regulatory restrictions we first have to navigate before we bring these products to market.

The potent combination of CBD and THC is being investigated, or has been used, to treat a range of conditions and specific diseases including: gastrointestinal conditions, phantom limb pain, migraines and common headaches, hypertension, and more.

Although the most common, a CBD-THC formula is far from the only combination of cannabinoids that can be used to treat different disorders. In fact, here's a partial list of combinations being considered as possible adjunct treatments for different specific conditions and diseases. (Consult with your doctor about the potential and current research on these for a particular illness you may be experiencing.)

The compounds listed below are based on the footnoted sources.

CBD plus:

- CBN, THCA, and THCV: *childhood epilepsy such as Dravet syndrome or Lennox-Gastaut syndrome (LGS)*[31]

- CBC, CBG, and THC: *clinical depression, muscular dystrophy.*[32]

- CBN and THC: *fibromyalgia*[33]

---

31. Emilio Perucca, "Cannabinoids in the Treatment of Epilepsy: Hard Evidence at Last?" *Journal of Epilepsy Research* 7, no. 2 (December 2017): 61–76. https://www.ncbi.nlm.nih.gov/pmc/articles /PMC5767492/.

32. Konieczny and Wilson, *Healing With CBD*, 64.

33. Konieczny and Wilson, *Healing With CBD*, 64

- THC and THCA: *Crohn's disease*[34]
- THCV: *diabetes mellitus*[35]
- CBC, CBG, CBN, THC, and THCA: *Lou Gehrig's disease or ALS (amyotrophic lateral sclerosis)*[36]
- CBC, CBG, THC, and THCA: *Parkinson's disease*[37]

If you decide you'd like to explore leveraging the entourage effect in your skincare regimen, read the label of any product extremely closely and consult your doctor first. The accepted practice for medical cannabis is to "start low and go slow." Start with the isolated CBD in organic topical products before advancing to those that

---

34. Rameshprabu Nallathambi, et al., "Anti-Inflammatory Activity in Colon Models Is Derived from Δ9-Tetrahydrocannabinolic Acid That Interacts with Additional Compounds in *Cannabis* Extracts," *Cannabis and Cannabinoid Research* 2, no. 1 (2017): 167–182. https://www.ncbi.nlm.nih.gov/pubmed/29082314.

35. Edward T. Wargent, et al., "The Cannabinoid Δ9-tetrahydrocannabivarin (THCV) Ameliorates Insulin Sensitivity in Two Mouse Models of Obesity," *Nutrition & Diabetes* 3, e68 (2013): n.p., https://doi.org/10.1038/nutd.2013.9.

36. Konieczny and Wilson, *Healing With CBD*, 64; Leinow and Birnbaum, *CBD: A Patient's Guide*, 93.

37. Helen Turner et al., "Cannabinoid Therapeutics in Parkinson's Disease: Promise and Paradox," *Journal of Herbs, Spices & Medicinal Plants* 3 (2017): 231–248, https://doi.org/10.1080/10496475.2017.1312724.

combine CBD with THC or any combination of other cannabinoids.

You can also begin to add in vaping or oral ingestion in conjunction with a topical formula. To avoid unwanted side effects, I highly recommend consulting a certified medical professional who can help you safely and wisely integrate CBD into your health regimen. Refer to Chapter 5 for caution in regard to vaping.

Terpenes

The entourage effect can also come into play with many of the other potentially beneficial compounds in *Cannabis sativa*, such as *terpenes* and *flavonoids*. Terpenes provide odor and flavor to plants and fruits of all kinds and are present in relatively small amounts in cannabis. Terpenes are a fast-emerging area of research because they appear to offer multiple health benefits and are natural complements to both CBD and CBD-THC formulations. In fact, they offer such promise that they are being increasingly touted as potential dietary supplements in isolation. The most common of these terpenes include:

- Pinene. This is the most common terpene in nature and is present in citrus plants, conifers, cannabis, basil, rosemary, dill, and other plants. As the name indicates, the smell brings to mind pine or turpentine. It fights bacteria, reduces inflammation, and enhances memory. Just as important, pinene moderates some of the psychoactive effects of THC—most pointedly short-term memory loss—making it a good addition to any formula seeking to take advantage of the entourage effect. This terpene is also useful in combatting simple respiratory problems like congestion or a cold. In fact, a 2011 study described in the journal *Molecules* showed that pinene offers protective benefits for the lungs, especially in fighting viral infections.[38] Many strains of *Cannabis sativa* are cultivated to grow with high levels of pinene because of this terpene's many benefits and appealing aroma.

- Linalool. Whereas pinene can contribute to alertness, linalool is a sedative agent and is also effective at reducing inflammation, anxiety, and pain. Linalool is marked by a pleasing floral scent and can be found in lavender, coriander, birch, rosewood, and over one hundred other plants. Linalool's amazing potential as a standalone compound was captured in a 2016 study published in the journal *Neuropharmacology*; the study showed that this compound had

38. Zhiwei Yang, et al., "Comparative Anti-Infectious Bronchitis Virus (IBV) Activity of (-)-Pinene: Effect on Nucleocapsid (N) Protein," *Molecules* 16, no. 2 (February 2011): 1044–54, https://doi.org/10.3390/molecules16021044.

beneficial effects in reversing some symptoms of Alzheimer's in mice.[39] The sedative properties make this terpene a good addition to a stress-relief regimen as well as an excellent complement to any sleep aid formula.

- Beta-caryophyllene. One of the most abundant terpenes in cannabis, beta-caryophyllene has a spicy, woodsy aroma and is found in cloves, hops, Thai basil, and oregano among other herbs and flowering plants. This is one of the most potentially important terpenes because it directly activates cannabinoid receptors, mimicking the role of a cannabinoid—most specifically on CB2 receptors in immune tissues throughout the body. Trials involving black pepper essential oils rich in B-caryophyllene have been shown to curb nicotine cravings in comparison to a placebo. The terpene is also a potential addiction treatment and shows promise in reducing symptoms of peptic ulcers and depression, as well as relieving pain, inflammation, and gastrointestinal tract issues. A 2014 article in the journal *Pharmacology*

39. Angélica Maria Sabogal-Guáqueta, Edison Osorio, and Gloria Patricia Cardona-Gómez, "Linalool Reverses Neuropathological and Behavioral Impairments in Old Triple Transgenic Alzheimer's Mice," *Neuropharmacology* 102 (March 2016): 111–20, https://doi.org/10.1016/j.neuropharm.2015.11.002.

described how B-caryophyllene activated cannabinoid receptors including CB2 and PPAR, reducing symptoms of Alzheimer's in mice.[40] This terpene has been recognized by the FDA as a safe food additive and supplement.

- Myrcene. This key component in cannabis plays a role in the distinctive smell of the plant, and the aroma is considered earthy and musky. In addition to cannabis, myrcene can be found in citrus, herbs such as basil, thyme, and lemongrass, and mangoes. Myrcene is thought to assist cannabinoids in crossing the blood-brain barrier, facilitating the joint and deep-tissue therapeutic effect of compounds such as CBD and CBN. Myrcene fights bacteria, fungus, and inflammation.

- Limonene. Limonene is largely responsible for the fresh smell and some of the taste of oranges, and is concentrated in orange rinds. It can also be found in peppermint, rosemary, and juniper. The scent is so appealing that limonene is used as an additive in both cleaning products and cosmetics. It is con-

---

40. Yujie Cheng, Sha Liu, and Zhi Dong, "β-Caryophyllene Ameliorates the Alzheimer-like Phenotype in APP/PS1 Mice Through CB2 Receptor Activation and the PPARγ Pathway," *Pharmacology* 94, no. 1–2 (September 2014): 1–12, https://doi .org/10.1159/000362689.

sidered a mood elevator, a digestive aid (useful in relieving heartburn and acid reflux), an antidepressant, and an anxiety fighter. Limonene also helps other terpenes absorb through the skin and mucosa. Medical researchers suspect that limonene may play a role in blocking carcinogens from damaging cells, and the compound has killed cancer cells in the laboratory.[41] However, clinical studies are needed to clarify the potential role this terpene may play in preventing or fighting cancer.[42] (A 2012 study published in the journal *Human & Experimental Toxicology* found that limonene inhibited tumor growth in lab mice.[43])

- Humulene. Originally classified as alpha-caryophyllene, humulene is related to beta-caryophyllene. It

---

41. Xiao Yu, et al., "d-Limonene Exhibits Antitumor Activity by Inducing Autophagy and Apoptosis in Lung Cancer," *Onco Targets and Therapy* 11 (April 2018): 1833–47, https://doi.org/10.2147/OTT.S155716.

42. Xiao-Guang Lu, et al., "Inhibition Of Growth And Metastasis of Human Gastric Cancer Implanted in Nude Mice by d-Limonene," *World Journal of Gastroenterology* 10, no. 14 (July 2004): 2140–44, https://www.ncbi.nlm.nih.gov/pmc/articles/PMC4572353/.

43. S. C. Chaudhary, et al., "d-Limonene Modulates Inflammation, Oxidative Stress and Ras-ERK Pathway to Inhibit Murine Skin Tumorigenesis," *Human & Experimental Toxicology* 31, no. 8 (February 2012): 798–811, https://doi.org/10.1177/0960327111434948.

has a similar earthy, spicy aroma and is considered largely responsible for the rich smell of hops. Humulene is also found in basil, coriander, and clove. As an isolated ingredient, it has long been used in traditional Chinese medicine. But even in the West, the antibacterial, anti-inflammatory, and appetite-suppressing properties of humulene are well known and accepted. However, perhaps the most exciting frontier for this terpene lies in cancer fighting. A study published in 2016 in the journal *Cancer Medicine*,[44] as well as an earlier 2003 study published in *Planta Medica*,[45] point to the potential for humulene as a tumor and cancer-cell antagonist.

- Eucalyptol. This terpene gets its name from eucalyptus; it's a primary agent of the distinctive smell of the tree and leaves. It is also found in tea trees, bay leaves, and mugwort. The bracing, somewhat energizing aroma is why eucalyptol is used in mouthwash and cough suppressants such as lozenges. It

44. Klaudyna Fidyt, et al., "β-caryophyllene and β-caryophyllene Oxide—Natural Compounds of Anticancer and Analgesic Properties," *Cancer Medicine* 5, no. 10 (October 2016): 3007–17, https://doi.org/10.1002/cam4.816.

45. Jean Legault, et al., "Antitumor Activity of Balsam Fir Oil: Production of Reactive Oxygen Species Induced by alpha-Humulene as Possible Mechanism of Action," *Planta Medica* 69, no. 5 (May 2003): 402–07, https://doi.org/10.1055/s-2003-39695.

has been used for neuropathic pain relief and provides a cooling sensation—both of which could be
useful in topical preparations for use on skin conditions. It also significantly enhances absorption of
other topical formula ingredients and consequently
may facilitate the penetration of CBD into skin layers. Eucalyptol may provide significant pain relief.
This terpene is an antibacterial, antifungal, antioxidant, and antiproliferative—meaning it may slow the
growth of cells, specifically in cancer tumors. Its role
in inhibiting colon tumor growth was highlighted
in a study published in *Oncology Reports* in 2013.[46]
Eucalyptol is also known to provide both stress relief
and alertness.

- Terpineol. Found in lilac, pine trees, lime blossoms,
and more than a hundred other plants, terpineol
shows promise in easing withdrawal symptoms and
reducing tolerance buildup of opioids such as mor-
phine. In fact, it is being used in combination with
CBD and beta-caryophyllene to treat addiction.
Although not as powerful as some other terpenes,
terpineol is considered a mild anti-inflammatory,

---

46. Soichiro Murata, et al., "Antitumor Effect of 1, 8-cineole Against
Colon Cancer," *Oncology Reports* 30, no. 6 (December 2013):
2647–52, https://doi.org/10.3892/or.2013.2763.

antioxidant, antibiotic, and antiproliferative, and it offers sedative effects.

Flavonoids

Flavonoids are compounds that give plants and fruits their characteristic colors and flavors. They are found in vegetables, fruits such as berries and apples, soybeans, tea, red wine, and a wide variety of plants. As with terpenes, flavonoids offer some health benefits. Flavonoids are abundant in cannabis plants. Studies have shown that flavonoids offer significant cardiovascular and nervous system protection, as well as anti-inflammatory, antioxidant, antibacterial, and cancer-fighting properties similar in strength to terpenes.[47]

There are more than eight thousand flavonoids in nature. Around twenty have been identified in cannabis. They are found throughout the plant's leaves, seeds, and flowers. They may be most effective used in conjunction with terpenes and cannabinoids to optimize the entourage effect.

Flavonoids are currently being investigated for their potential in making other compounds available to the body—a process known as *bioavailability*. They also help move agents like CBD down through all the layers of the

---

47. Mariam Abotaleb, et al., "Flavonoids in Cancer and Apoptosis," *Cancers* 11, no. 1 (January 2019): 28, https://doi.org/10.3390 /cancers11010028.

skin, which is known as *transdermal transport*. This line of research holds special promise for dermatology, allergy treatment, and rheumatology.

A group of flavonoids known as cannaflavins are found exclusively in cannabis plants and offer potent anti-inflammatory properties. A brief overview of individual flavonoids includes:

- Apigenin. Found in abundance in a variety of fruits and vegetables such as grapes, apples, and parsley, apigenin has been used for centuries in traditional Chinese medicine. That ancient culture hit on a winner: This flavonoid has well-chronicled, strong anti-inflammatory, antibacterial, antiviral, antioxidant, and other properties. It has been used in applications as diverse as lowering blood pressure and to reduce side effects from strong anti-rejection drugs used in organ transplants. But perhaps the greatest area of promise lies in apigenin's potential cancer-fighting properties. It has shown broad anti-cancer effects in a number of studies, including one published in the *International Journal of Cancer* in 2000. That study showed that the flavonoid (in the laboratory) inhibited melanoma cell growth and induced death of those cells.[48]

- Kaempferol. This is another standard ingredient in traditional Chinese medicine (usually contained in fruits or flowers such as peach tree blossoms). The flavonoid is also found in green tea, the brassica family of vegetables, apples, grapefruit, and many other fruits and vegetables. It has been used along with a group of compounds to treat depression and proactively head off heart disease caused by inflammation. Like many other flavonoids, this one fights bacteria, viruses, and inflammation. Of particular interest, though, is kaempferol's potential as a skin protector. A 2010 study published in the *International Journal of Dermatology* described its role in slowing skin photoaging caused by UVB exposure.[49] There is some evidence that kaempferol may have cancer-fighting properties, as well.

---

48. Sara Caltagirone, et al., "Flavonoids Apigenin and Quercetin Inhibit Melanoma Growth and Metastatic Potential," *International Journal of Cancer* 87, no. 4 (July 2000): 595–600, https://doi.org/10.1002/1097-0215(20000815)87:4<595::AID-IJC21>3.0.CO;2-5.

49. Hye Min Park, et al., "Extract of *Punica granatum* Inhibits Skin Photoaging Induced by UVB Irradiation," *International Journal of Dermatology* 49, no. 3 (March 2010): 276–82, https://doi.org/10.1111/j.1365-4632.2009.04269.x.

- Quercetin. Featuring a distinctively bitter flavor, quercetin is a common dietary supplement. As with most flavonoids, it is found in a range of plants including cherries, citrus fruits, tomatoes, black tea, and in abundance in kale. This is perhaps the most widely researched flavonoid and has been shown to have anti-allergenic, anti-inflammatory, antioxidant, cardio-protective, neuro-protective, and anti-cancer properties.[50] Quercetin has also been included in topical preparations using a lipid and silicone medium for delivery.

- Orientin. A potent antioxidant, orientin is found in many medicinal plants, as well as in bamboo leaves, passionflowers, and cannabis. Orientin has also shown a modest antiviral effect and a more significant impact on heart and vascular health. It also has neuroprotective qualities.

---

50. Jiyun Ahn, et al., "The Anti-obesity Effect of Quercetin Is Mediated by the AMPK and MAPK Signaling Pathways," *Biochemical and Biophysical Research Communications* 373, no. 4 (September 2008): 545–49, https://doi.org/10.1016/j.bbrc.2008.06.077; Dong-sheng Fan, et al., "Anti-inflammatory, Antiviral and Quantitative Study of Quercetin-3-O-β-D-Glucuronide in *Polygonum perfoliatum* L.," *Fitoterapia* 82, no. 6 (September 2011): 805–10, https://doi.org/10.1016/j.fitote.2011.04.007; A. P. Rogerio, et al., "Anti-inflammatory Activity of Quercetin and Isoquercitrin in Experimental Murine Allergic Asthma," *Inflammation Research* 56, no. 10 (October 2007): 402–08, https://doi.org/10.1007/s00011-007-7005-6.

- Luteolin. Another common dietary supplement sold in capsules, luteolin is found in bark, mint, and brassica vegetables such as broccoli. This flavonoid is often combined with others for a synergistic effect. The broad range of benefits associated with luteolin include immune system support and anti-inflammatory, antioxidant, antimicrobial, and cancer-fighting effects.

- Beta-sitosterol. Unique among flavonoids, beta-sitosterol is similar in structure to fatty acids and is derived from a wide range of vegetables, nuts, and seeds (and has just recently been isolated from the cannabis plant). It has been used in the treatment of prostate diseases and menopause and can reduce cholesterol and prevent heart disease. Its chemical structure makes beta-sitosterol an excellent ingredient for skin creams because it's a moisturizer and can soothe inflamed skin.

Terpenes and flavonoids are available as supplements, but they are usually only present in trace amounts in CBD oil. So, for now, we will concentrate on CBD itself.

CBD can be a powerful part of an entourage of cannabinoids, but it's important to keep in mind that CBD alone has potent properties all on its own. It can have a noticeably positive effect on both your skin and general health.

5 · CBD DELIVERY OPTIONS

I STRONGLY RECOMMEND CONSULTING your physician or a medical practitioner certified and knowledgeable in the application and use of medical marijuana prior to starting any ongoing course of CBD no matter what delivery method you choose. Even though CBD capsules and topical skincare formulas are available over the counter, it's wise to ask your doctor if using CBD will interfere with any prescription drug or supplement you might be taking. CBD should also be avoided to treat children or women who are pregnant or breastfeeding. Still, it's important to understand how safe CBD is. The World Health Organization found, "In humans, CBD exhibits no effects indicative of any abuse or dependence potential... To date, there is no evidence of … public health related problems associated with the use of pure CBD."[51]

Once you've decided to integrate CBD into your skincare and skin-health regimen, make sure you use the best product possible. I advise all my patients to use only the purest natural CBD oil you can find from the most reputable source. Because CBD is a compound closely related to those created within our own bodies, the closer the CBD is to its natural state, the more likely it is to have a positive effect on the body.

For the same reason, I strongly caution against synthetic versions of CBD or any cannabinoid unless designed and approved as medicine, such as Nabilone for treatment of nausea. There are many illegal "designer drugs"—one of the most notorious is "Spice"—that have been responsible for several deaths. Natural CBD is perfectly suited for your body's ECS, the network of receptors, neurotransmitters, and enzymes that maintains healthy balance. Synthetic CBD and THC are not. Synthetic versions are famously unpredictable, and it's difficult to know if they contain contaminants or unhealthy additives.

---

51. Expert Committee on Drug Dependence, *Cannabidiol (CBD) Pre-Review Report, Agenda Item 5.2, Thirty-ninth Meeting* (Geneva, Switzerland: World Health Organization, November 2017), 5, https://www.who.int/medicines/access/controlled-substances/5.2 _CBD.pdf.

As the popularity of CBD has exploded, so has the number of products that contain less than what is claimed on the label. Sometimes the products contain none of what's claimed on the label! A study published in the Journal of American Medical Association revealed that more than 70 percent of CBD extracts sold online are mislabeled, and a significant number of those had less than 1 percent of CBD and contained impurities.[52] Impure CBD oil may be tainted by anything from murky carrier oils to solvents, resulting in potential harm to consumers. For my complete guidelines on how to shop for the best CBD and cannabinoid products, see Chapter 12.

Delivery Methods

When it comes to taking care of your skin or treating skin disorders with CBD, there are basically four delivery methods: oral, inhalation, sublingual, or topical. (Undiluted CBD oil is rarely used to treat any condition because the consistency and smell—and even the texture—are rather unpleasant.) A key factor among these is "bioavailability": how fast the dose makes it into your system and how much CBD actually makes it into the bloodstream.

---

52. Marcel O. Bonn-Miller, Mallory J. E. Loflin, and Brian F. Thomas, "Labeling Accuracy of Cannabidiol Extracts Sold Online," *JAMA* 318, no. 17 (November 2017): 1708–09, https://doi.org/10.1001/jama.2017.11909.

- Oral. CBD is orally ingested in capsules and edibles, with the CBD suspended in a medium such as olive oil, sesame oil, or gummies. I like capsules because the dosing is accurate and you can control release by scheduling when you consume the capsules. Capsules come in oil-filled or dried residue versions; I don't believe there is a significant difference in effectiveness between the two. Edibles have a famously bad reputation for precision in dosing, but products such as gummies produced by medical marijuana clinics (if legal where you live) contain precise amounts of CBD. This should be listed on the label. You'll know exactly how much you're getting with each piece you consume. Some people also find edibles easier and more pleasant to take.

  In either case, however, there will be a significant lag before the CBD reaches your bloodstream because of the slow and erratic processes of digestion and metabolism through our stomach, intestines, and liver.

  For that same reason, the amount of active CBD that makes it into your system will be less than what's in the ingestible form because your stomach acids will destroy some of the CBD. A study in the journal *Chemistry & Biodiversity* estimated that only between 4 and 20 percent of an ingested cannabinoid makes it into the bloodstream.[53] However, keep in mind that the percentage will vary based on personal factors. For instance, if you are on a regular course of over-the-counter or prescription medication to treat GERD or acid reflux, you probably have a minute amount of gastric acid in your gut. This will allow for a higher absorption of CBD from oral ingestion than in a person taking no antacids or acid reflux medications.

However, nothing is ever that simple when it comes to our gut and digestion. There are other physiological factors that affect digestion speed. These include certain drugs, diabetes, inflammatory bowel diseases, acute and chronic infections, sedentary lifestyle, gastric surgeries due to peptic ulcer disease, and obesity. This is not an exhaustive list, but the point is to understand your own system and make informed decisions in consultation with your medical professionals as to how and how much CBD to take.

Liver enzymes such as cytochrome P450 also play a pivotal role in how much CBD makes it into your bloodstream after going through your intestines.

53. Marilyn A. Huestis, "Human Cannabinoid Pharmacokinetics," *Chemistry & Biodiversity* 4, no. 8 (August 2007): 1770–1804, https://doi.org/10.1002/cbdv.200790152.

This is known as "first pass metabolism." (The same enzymes affect how well you handle your alcohol.) To make matters even more complicated, genetic mutations in this complex of enzymes are not uncommon, which will further slow down or speed up metabolism. In this exciting era of genetic testing, a blood test can identify the need to exercise caution or to avoid altogether certain drugs such as statins, anti-hypertension medications, muscle relaxers, and blood thinners. The vast majority of prescribed or over-the-counter drugs and supplements rely on P450 and will compete with oral CBD, which may significantly alter the bioavailability and the effects of each on our bodies.

- Inhalation. There are two ways to inhale CBD or other cannabinoids: smoking and vaping. As a physician, I counsel my patients to be very cautious with both. With smoking, you do not know how much CBD you're getting, and you could breathe in toxins along with the smoke. Many manufacturers now offer CBD vaping pods with precise doses of the cannabinoid that can be carried in a fairly benign medium. You'll inhale more steam than smoke, which is less damaging to your lungs than smoking. Vaping allows quick consumption of high doses of CBD, and it enters the bloodstream almost immediately. Obviously, this makes sense for certain conditions and not for others. Vaping has shown real effectiveness in relieving both itching and pain—two key exacerbating factors in most serious skin conditions. However, as I write this, there is growing medical attention around, and caution against, vaping with or without cannabinoids. There have been numerous lung-related injuries and several deaths. The cause is likely due to many factors, and I suspect it involves chemical additives. Still, I urge extreme caution when inhaling any substance. Keep abreast of medical news, purchase your CBD from state-regulated growers and manufacturers, and vape only under the care of physician specialists.

- Sublingual. You've most likely heard of "tinctures," formulas containing cannabinoids in a nontoxic carrier medium such as oil. Generally, sublingual doses are taken by dropping a set amount of a tincture under your tongue. Medical marijuana clinics and health food stores, where legal, offer CBD tinctures in precise doses as well as different ratios of CBD to THC. It is simple to use the supplied dropper—which often is marked with milliliter measurements—to take the dose you prefer. As with inhaling, the CBD hits your bloodstream almost immediately, and none is lost to stomach acids. I like the idea of CBD tinctures because they are easy to control and very quick to work. More and more, they are also available in flavors such as mint or lemon. That makes them easier to tolerate for people who don't like putting oily drops in their mouth. Keep in mind the proper way to take sublingual liquids. Allow absorption to take place with a few drops at a time under the tongue for the most effective bioavailability.

- Topical. Where general skincare is concerned, topical applications containing CBD are the most common method of delivery. The challenge with topical applications is controlling the dosage, so carefully testing any formulation on your body is key. Start by using the product in a small test patch that will be hidden by clothing. Apply a light amount of any topical preparation, increasing thickness and frequency of application until you achieve the effects you're after. Fortunately, there are a remarkable number of topical products on the market. For instance, you will find basic skin creams and sunscreens with CBD, as well as makeup products, acne-fighting formulations, and more. It is important to note that topical applications of CBD creams and lotions typically do not pass into the bloodstream. They affect only the top layers of the skin. The reason this is such a crucial point is that it means you can use a formulation that includes both CBD and THC without getting high. Depending on the skin condition you're treating, the combination can be more effective (especially in curbing pain and itching) than CBD alone. In fact, in my own beauty company, Aethera, we are exploring ways to combine THC and CBD to increase the effectiveness of our products.

On the other hand, some salves and balms, such as those developed for arthritis and joint pain, are formulated with a carrier that can cross the skin-blood barrier. The most effective way to deliver these doses is with a transdermal patch. Worn like the nicotine patch long used by smokers attempting to quit, a transdermal CBD patch can be placed in a discreet location on the body for a sustained-release dose of the cannabinoid. These patches come in CBD alone and in combination with THC and even other cannabinoids to leverage the entourage effect. In most cases, the CBD is absorbed into the bloodstream in fifteen to thirty minutes, and the release will last eight to twelve hours. Often recommended for arthritis and other joint conditions and pain, these are specifically meant to penetrate into the lower tissue and muscle past the skin-blood barrier and will carry the CBD—and THC if appropriate—into the bloodstream. It's essential to read labels and understand not only how much CBD is in the product but also what type of carrier medium is used. I generally advise people to only use transdermal patches under the supervision of a physician or professional well versed in the use of medical cannabis.

CBD Delivery Methods and Absorption Times

Delivery Method	Uptake	Duration
Oral	30–90 minutes	3.5–6 hours
Inhalation	Within seconds to minutes	1–3 hours
Sublingual	Within seconds to minutes	3–6 hours
Topical	20–45 minutes	6–8 hours
Suppository	Approx. 15 minutes	6–8 hours

Refining Delivery

Many people supplement topical CBD use with other forms of ingestion. Sublingual tinctures are great ways to deliver exact doses into your system. CBD oil capsules are more common for other health conditions and general health maintenance, but they can certainly be used to supplement topical formulas for skin conditions. The one problem with oral ingestion is, of course, that some of the curative power of the CBD is lost as it is processed by stomach acid and filtered through the liver.

Although most people are put off by the delivery system, if you are hoping to use CBD in a clinical way to mitigate symptoms from serious conditions such as Crohn's disease, severe nausea, and certain cancers, you can turn to rectal suppositories. (Suppositories, like transdermal patches, should only be used under the supervision of a qualified medical professional.) This is actually a highly efficient delivery method, one that bypasses the filtering mechanism of the stomach (acids) and liver (biochemical) to deliver maximum dosage right to the rectum and large intestine and into the bloodstream. The bioavailability of CBD through this method is extremely fast thanks to the large intestine's porous membrane. As a bonus, a combination of CBD and THC delivered through suppository greatly diminishes—if not eliminates—the intoxicating effect of the THC. Suppositories are best suited for those who are unable to tolerate or have preference against other delivery methods.

Adjusting Dose

Whatever method you choose, finding the right dosage for you and the condition or disease you're treating is a matter of fine tuning. No academic, medical, or government body has set dosage parameters for CBD, or even for CBD-THC combinations. Because this is a natural compound impacting a system that varies from body to body, the correct dosage will depend on physical size, weight, BMI (body mass index), medical history, your own particular tolerance and metabolism, genetic makeup, and other factors.

Titration is a word you'll hear often in discussions or writing about CBD dosage. That's a scientific word meaning incremental increases, slowly over time, generously allowing for necessary adjustment. It's the method that I, and most doctors working with medical cannabis, recommend. Start at a low dose and slowly build it up until you hit the "sweet spot" of efficacy for your purposes.

Dosing is complicated slightly by the fact that CBD and other cannabinoids are *biphasic*. That means that their efficiency follows a bell curve. Too high a dose may have the same effect as too low a dose. The biphasic nature of these compounds is why you can sometimes get a better outcome by reducing the amount of CBD if increasing the dose is not having the desired effect.

Keep in mind that our bodies build up a tolerance to cannabinoids. The appropriate dose may change over time, so it's wise to keep a close eye on your response to CBD and adjust the dosage if the effect changes. You always want to be somewhere under the bell curve, not on either side. I counsel all my patients using medical cannabis, or just CBD, to regularly take periods without the CBD or any cannabis product in their systems. Abstaining for two to seven days will completely clear out your system and reset your metabolism and ensure that you never experience the side effect known as "CBD hyperemesis syndrome" (see Chapter 9).

There are three basic levels of dosages but, in reality, dosing is a much more gradated process. Understandably, these are very flexible, wide ranges that allow for the variations I've discussed above. Generally, regardless of the dose you're taking, it's broken down into two times a day or more.

- Microdosing: This is modest maintenance for general health and well-being. Microdosing is a good place for people to start if they just want some of the general benefits of CBD, such as anti-inflammatory and better sleep. The range is roughly 1 mg to 20 mg per day. I recommend a starting dose at 2 mg to 2.5 mg.

- Medium dosing: This is the range in which I start most patients using CBD to treat simple rashes or other moderate skin or health conditions. I think 20 to 100 mgs is a reasonable starting point for anyone who is not hypersensitive or inexperienced to CBD. It is also a common dose range for ongoing health maintenance.

- Macrodosing: Just as it sounds, this is a very large dose usually reserved for severe, perhaps life-threatening diseases such as cancer. This level of CBD should never be taken without medical supervision. The range goes from 100 mgs to 800 mgs and beyond. However, it's worth mentioning that for some more serious conditions, medical practitioners well versed in medical cannabis may prescribe much higher doses. Mega-doses have not been studied in humans and should not ever be considered without consultation with physician specialists experienced in the application of medical cannabis.

Whatever dose you begin with, try it for five to seven days before making a change. If you aren't achieving the effect you want, increase the dose incrementally, trying the new dose for another five to seven days. In the event you experience unwanted effects, back down to the previous dose for a week. Experiment until you achieve the right dose for you and your body.

Given the proliferation of over-the-counter formulas containing CBD (not to mention CBD capsules sold nationwide), it's easy to jump right into using the cannabinoid. But I always counsel anyone to check with your physician first. CBD can act as a competitive inhibitor of cytochrome P450, the liver enzyme that synthesizes many prescription drugs. That's why CBD can mess with the uptake of certain medications. Of particular concern, CBD can amplify the effects of anti-depressants, pain relievers, sedatives, and muscle relaxants. It can also work the other way; for instance, many cannabinoids can interact with the diabetic drug Metformin and make it less effective. Simple topical formulas containing CBD are far less likely to have an effect one way or another on prescription drugs because lotions and creams are not likely to penetrate the skin-blood barrier.

One last caveat: before using a combination of CBD and THC, check with your primary physician or CBD specialist for any medical conditions or medications that are contraindicated or may lead to adverse interactions. And, of course, in no instance should you break the law; always check if cannabis and specific cannabinoids are legal in your state.

6 · OUR WONDROUS SKIN

I HAVE A FAVORITE mantra in my intensive care unit: "Observation before palpation." It means I want to take a close look at a patient before I act. That often involves studying the patient's skin—and the skin can tell quite a story. The skin is the body's most visible organ, so discoloration or breaks in its integrity reveal a lot about our inner health journey. My patients are often plagued by dry, peeling, and itchy skin due to severe nutritional deficiency in response to acute and chronic illnesses. Others suffer red rashes from reactions to antibiotics or chemicals in body wash, or they deal with wounds formed by undue pressures on the skin from prolonged immobilization. These skin conditions can be painful. They add to the suffering of patients already enduring pain and discomfort from whatever condition caused them to be hospitalized in the first place.

As I have embarked on the search for nontoxic tools to lessen suffering and heal the body, I get more and more excited about the potential role of CBD, cannabinoids, and other compounds of the cannabis plant. Skin health is not skin deep, nor is the relationship we have with our skin one way. As the skin protects us, we need to understand how to protect our skin. Because the following may be a bit technical, I will highlight key components of our skin matrix and suggest how CBD and cannabinoids fit into our overall self-care.

The story of your skin is being written as you read this. This barrier between you and the outside world is constantly regenerating itself, staying strong as your body's first line of defense. Unlike other organs in your body, the skin is continuously fending off insults, trauma, and damage from both internal sources like poor nutrition, stress, and a compromised immune system, and external factors such as the sun, allergens, and minor bumps and cuts. Perhaps the most detrimental of all is the sun. The sun's damaging UV rays find you almost anywhere you stand or sit. Of course, your skin is also your largest organ, comprising 15 to 20 percent of body weight, which means that there's a lot more of it to damage. If you're reading this book, you may be already aware of much of this.

But what you might not know is what's happening at the cellular level: damage that speeds up aging, makes your entire system more vulnerable to infection, and increases your risk of cancer. The great news is that there are tens of thousands of research studies and peer-reviewed papers exploring the medicinal benefits of CBD, THC, and other cannabinoids in the quest for nontoxic self-care.[54] CBD boosts the immune system, fights inflammation, and has antioxidant and neuroprotective powers. Those are covered elsewhere in this book. Of course, CBD is not a panacea for all problems, and we need to apply a healthy dose of skepticism to the miraculous CBD claims in media reports and advertisements.

The following primer outlines the building blocks of what we think of as the body's outer layer. Any defect or disruption in the normal functioning of these layers—and the cells within—will lead to disease, accelerate aging, and cause pain and suffering. When our own naturally-produced cannabinoids—which bind to CB1 and CB2 receptors—are ineffective or insufficient, external applications and use of cannabinoids such as CBD

---

54. Americans for Safe Access, "Medical Marijuana Access in the United States: A Patient-Focused Analysis of the Patchwork of State Laws," (Washington, DC), 2018 Annual Report, n.d., https:// american-safe-access.s3.amazonaws.com/sos2018/2018_State_of _the_States_Report_web.pdf.

potentially play powerful roles in healing. Keep in mind that many factors, including our individual and unique genetic makeup, will affect your individual response to CBD. That's why I recommend partnering with a medical doctor who has experience in, and knowledge of, using medical cannabis.

Skin Structure

The skin is composed of three layers. Starting from the outside in, they are the relatively thin top layer *epidermis*, the much thicker middle layer *dermis*, and the irregular base of *subcutaneous fat*. These layers are, like the rest of our body, in a continual process of dying, regenerating, and repair. Within each layer there are many different types of cells performing a wide range of functions. For what appears on the surface as a very simple, unified structure, the construction of each layer in the skin is amazingly complex.

The endocannabinoid system (ECS) that I discussed in Chapter 3 helps regulate the life cycle of every skin cell, ensuring efficient cell turnover and protecting against the most devastating of diseases. Although we think of our skin as delicate and easily penetrated (how often have you accidently cut yourself?), the skin's healing response to wounds and injury is incredible. More importantly, the skin seals out the vast majority of contaminants in our environment. To make it past the various layers and cells of the skin and into the bloodstream, a compound must either be a unique combination of fat-soluble and water-soluble components, or it must be so microscopically small that passing through is like water passing through the finest fabric.

First Level—The Epidermis: Five Layers

The epidermis is our waterproof barrier against the world. This layer is also what gives us our skin tone and contributes so much to how we look. It not only prevents infection from outside agents, it inhibits water loss through the skin to slow dehydration. Of course, the epidermis is also our first line of defense against the sun's UV rays. This layer is not uniform—it is thicker or thinner depending on the part of the body. But despite being thin relative to the other strata of your skin, this layer can be further broken down into four additional discreet layers of cells.

Starting from the innermost layer, the *stratum basale* is full of basal cells in the continual process of dividing and pushing up toward the surface. This layer holds the *melanin*, the skin's pigment, that is so important in response to UV light damage. A thin layer just under the stratum basale exists only on the palms of your hands and the soles of your feet—it's called the *stratum lucidem*, lending increased protection from damage due to friction. The amount and distribution of melanin throughout these cells determines skin color and tone. The stratum basale is attached to a basement membrane that holds the epidermis to the dermis by what are known as *hemidesmosomes*, and the cells in the epidermis are held together with similar molecular "glue" called *desmosomes*—the point of attack for autoimmune diseases, such as lupus, that affect the skin. Autoimmune diseases are illnesses that mistakenly trigger attacks on our healthy tissues and organs, resulting in inflammation, pain, and more illness.

The *stratum spinosum* is the squamous-cell layer where all the up-pushing basal cells turn into what are known as *keratinocytes*. Those cells produce keratin, an essential protective coating for skin, hair, and nails. This layer also contains cells that help regulate immune-system response: specialized cells that attach to foreign substances to prevent those contaminants from infiltrating the bloodstream.

The *stratum granulosum* is a migration layer where keratinocytes harden and dry out.

The *stratum corneum* is the topmost layer, full of dead keratinocytes in the process of being shed. Complete cell lifespan, from dividing in the bottom layer to shedding off the top, averages around twenty-eight days. The layer blocks pathogens through a network of lipids, acids, hydrolytic enzymes, and defensive antimicrobial peptides. Problems can occur in any of the sublayers and at any time in the life cycle of the epidermal cells.

We care about the cells in the epidermis because most skin cancers begin in this layer, and it suffers near-constant injury from UV rays. By gaining insight into how our skin is under ongoing attack, we can arm ourselves with the best defense.

The Four Cell Types in the Epidermis

The epidermis contains four basic cell types. *Keratinocytes* are the building blocks that define the life cycle of the epidermis. They are present in all four layers and make up about 95 percent of the cells in the epidermis. Keratinocytes are actually called different names as they rise through the epidermis layers, gaining keratin, flattening, and maturing. From the bottom up, they are *basal cells*, *prickle cells*, *squamous cells*, and a top, dead layer of *keratin*. Regular and gentle exfoliation of keratin keeps the pores from clogging with harmful bacteria, which could lead to conditions such as acne. CBD has roles in both decreasing inflammation and in curtailing the spread of harmful bacteria by decreasing, if not eliminating, the need to itch.

Melanocytes produce melanin, the pigment that colors your skin and helps protect the epidermis from UV ray damage. Melanin is inserted into keratinocytes as it travels to the top of our epidermis. CBD has shown promise in lessening the damaging effects from exposure to UV rays. Sunscreen, sunblock, and avoidance are all mainstays for protection from UV radiation exposure.

Langerhans cells are the front-line defense against allergens, irritants, and other attackers. They are responsible for recognizing these threats and breaking them down to be carried away as waste products. They also signal the immune system to send important immune response cells to the site of injury or insult. Our natural cannabinoids are also stimulated to locally inhibit the release of certain destructive proteins or pro-inflammatory cytokines. Topical CBD has additive benefits in this immune response on cytokines and healing.

Merkel cells coordinate with the nervous system to transmit light pressure sensations on the skin to our brain.

Second Level—The Dermis:
Two Sublayers and Extracellular Matrix

The dermis is where many skin conditions get their start because of the variety of structures and many complex functions that occur in this layer. It is sometimes referred to as the "true skin" because it is the topmost area where nutrients flow in and waste products flow out via blood capillaries.

The dermis can be further divided into two basic layers: the upper *papillary* dermis and a lower *reticular* dermis. Nerve endings are some of the most essential components of the dermis, transmitting pain and itch as well as the more subtle signals of temperature and pressure. This layer is where the elastin and collagen that keep skin supple and youthful are produced. In fact, the largest part of the dermis is the extracellular matrix (ECM), made up largely of collagen and elastin (they are called structural proteins because of their vital function in this layer), along with the *laminins* and *fibronectin* that serve as a glue for this layer, and *glycosaminoglycans*, sugar compounds that help retain essential moisture within the ECM. The dermis also contains sweat glands, called *eccrine*, which are vital for controlling body temperature. Sebaceous glands control the production of oil (called *sebum*) that can cause so many skin conditions and issues. Those glands are always attached to a hair follicle, another structure particular to the dermis.

Many problems on the surface of the skin start with dead cells—keratinocytes—clogging the sebaceous glands and trapping sebum, bacteria, and waste products. That detritus can wreak havoc with skin, especially when it clogs up the pores, and areas around the base of growing hair follicles. (Fun fact: tiny muscles at the base of hair follicles in the dermis are responsible for goose pimples; they tighten in response to fear or cold, creating small bulges on the surface!) The layer is also full of blood vessels that nourish the skin and help regulate body temperature.

As you can imagine, different areas of the body have different concentrations of each of these structures. The dermis contains a great deal of water and, when fully hydrated, adds a plump, youthful look to the skin. The dermis also communicates with the epidermis and can influence cell activity in that upper layer of skin. Skin aging is most dramatic in this layer.

The Five Cell Types of the Dermis

The dermis is a complicated, thicker layer with many cell types. *Mast cells* are another skin-defense mechanism, releasing histamines and other inflammatory chemicals and hormones whenever they sense damage in the tissue. *Macrophages* are large white blood cells, essentially immune cells that break down and remove some foreign bodies including viruses, bacteria, and even parasites, as well as waste material. Macrophages are essential to wound repair. *Pericytes* play a crucial role in blood-vessel formation and skin healing. *Fibroblasts* produce collagen and elastin and consequently aid in skin growth and repair. They are responsible for creating the connective framework for skin and healing wounds. *Pluripotential cells* reside at the base of hair follicles and function as stem cells—special structures that can become any other skin cell as necessary.

I had my own terrible experience with my dermis and epidermis when my moderate, painful reaction to hair dye erupted into a six-month, all-out war with my skin. Steroids could not quell the inflammation, antibiotics could not quickly kill the bacteria, and Tylenol did not eliminate my pain. However, I finally received the booster I needed to break my vicious cycle with topical CBD. An incidental benefit of the CBD and how it affected cells in the dermis was that I experienced brighter and more youthful-looking skin. Those wonderful results were why I worked with a lab to develop a CBD skincare line.

As we developed our products, I experimented with different formulations on my nurses, associates, family, and friends. I was pleasantly surprised that many told me they experienced a healthier feel and look. Several said the CBD serum took away puffiness and dark circles under their eyes and gave them a more youthful and healthy appearance. I believe this is a result of CBD's direct and indirect actions on the dermis.

For CBD to work most effectively, though, it must penetrate through the epidermis to the dermis.

Third Level—The Subcutaneous Fat

You can think of the subcutaneous fat like you would a jacket—it's the last line of protection for the body. The subcutaneous fat layer consists of *adipocytes*—fat cells. This layer also contains nerves and blood vessels. The fat stored in this layer creates a buffer to absorb the natural bumps and collisions the body goes through but also insulates the structure below the skin, helping maintain proper body temperature. A more important role—perhaps the most important role—is attaching the entire skin structure to muscle and bone. This layer serves as a conduit for the nerves and blood vessels in the dermis: they grow larger in this layer and are routed to other parts of the body.

It is important to stress that CBD and THC are hydrophobic, meaning they repel water. For either to be absorbed past the dermis and subcutaneous fat, these cannabinoids must be specially formulated into transdermal patches or some combination of water and lipid-soluble compounds. Doctors use this as a therapeutic treatment for localized joint or muscle pain management.

Skin Type

Many people, including medical professionals, assume that the darker skin associated with certain ethnic heritages means one is less likely to suffer from skin-related conditions and diseases. While it is true that darker skin is less prone to certain afflictions like skin cancer, anyone with skin can suffer from allergies, skin diseases such as psoriasis, and other common disorders. No matter what your "skin type," you have to take measures to care for and protect your skin. The sun's UV rays are the enemy of all skin, regardless of color. The factors affecting the health of your skin extend far beyond a type or a color and are complex.

However, understanding how professionals define skin type, and knowing the exact shade of your pigmentation, is a good—if crude—starting point. Professionals such as dermatologists use the Fitzpatrick scale to determine the right laser or light treatment for a given patient. Skin type will, if nothing else, affect to some degree the UV protection you need in given circumstances. (It will be part of your calculation of just how long you can rely on a particular sunblock or sunscreen to last.) To clarify skin type, a dermatologist named Thomas Fitzpatrick developed a scale of six skin types in 1975. The Fitzpatrick Scale is still in use today.

Fitzpatrick Skin Types

Type	UV Reaction	Characteristics
I	Always burns, never tans	Pale to pure white skin tone, Nordic or British ancestry, often coupled with blue, gray, or green eyes and red or blonde hair.
II	Usually burns, tans minimally	Cream-colored complexion with beige undertones, eyes may be any color
III	Sometimes mild burn, slow to tan	Ranging from golden, honey-colored to light olive skin
IV	Minimal burns, fast to tan	Mid-range brown skin, usually with dark eyes and hair

Type	UV Reaction	Characteristics
V	Rarely burns, easy tanning	From light to dark-brown sugar skin with dark hair and eyes
VI	Never burns	From dark brown to ebony, with dark to black eyes and hair

The other aspect to skin type is oily versus dry skin. Again, this is an overly simplistic breakdown. Keep in mind that your skin may be from 16 to 22 square feet (1.5 to 2 square meters) and is not the same all over. Some areas are much thicker than others, some have hair and some don't. Similarly, some regions of your skin may be excessively oily while other areas may be too dry. In addition, what you think may be an oily or dry skin condition could be the result of your local climate or even a consequence of something you regularly eat or drink (or something you don't).

It's always helpful in medicine—including preventive medicine—to quantify and codify biological differences. But my one issue with skin typing is that it can give people a false sense of security. I think it's more important to be informed about the impact external and internal factors can have on skin health and err on the side of caution when choosing preventive skincare practices. Interestingly, CBD and cannabinoids adjust to our variations by stimulating our endocannabinoid system to strike physiologic balance, healing sun-exposed skin, and helping new skin grow. However, our responses may vary significantly not only from one individual to another, but also in the same individual based on a host of factors including, but not limited to, cannabis usage, history, age, current intake of medication, or presence of other illnesses.

Another common mantra I preach to my patients and their families when they ask me "Why?" and "How?" is that there is no single cause or solution. The prescription always involves a well-devised care plan with multiple tools in the patient's own personal box. CBD and cannabinoids may be effective for your skin health and wellness. Again, I highly recommend consulting certified health care professionals who have expertise in medical cannabis.

7 · YOUR SKIN UNDER ATTACK

WE MUST BE AWARE every day of the risks to our skin health, starting with the sun and UV radiation exposure. The sun is the most significant external factor impacting your skin. It has both positive and negative effects. Sunlight on your skin can be a wonderful feeling, warming you and even causing a release of endorphins that relax you and add to a feeling of well-being. It also triggers a chemical in the epidermis to convert to vitamin D, an essential nutrient for bone growth and other functions. A sunny day is almost universally associated with happiness. But the sun's long-term effects on the skin can be anything but happy.

The problem is that benign, pleasant sunshine contains destructive ultraviolet (UV) rays. UV rays are a constant danger to skin—

and overall—health. UV rays attack and damage the DNA in skin cells, causing mutations, free radicals (highly charged electrons that cause damage throughout our bodies), and other waste products. Complicating the picture, there is not just one kind of UV ray in sunshine but two—UVA (long wave ultraviolet A) and UVB (short wave ultraviolet B); a third, UVC, doesn't play an important role in skin health. Think of the "A" as standing for "aging" and the "B" as standing for "burning."

UVA rays penetrate deeper into the dermis and are most frequently associated with premature skin aging and other long-term damage. They can also contribute to skin cancer development. UVB rays are stronger and don't penetrate as deeply but can damage skin-cell DNA in the epidermis. They are responsible for burns related to sun exposure and are strongly associated with melanoma and other skin cancers.

Both types are present at all times when the sun is shining. They are strongest during the middle of the day— from 10 a.m. to 4 p.m.—and in the spring and summer. But make no mistake: UV rays are present anytime during the day. The farther your location is from the equator, the weaker the UV rays that reach your skin—although damage from these rays remains a concern in regions as far north as Alaska. UV rays are stronger at higher altitudes, and the myth that cloud cover blocks UV radiation is just that—a mistaken assumption that leads to a lot of skin sun damage. Making matters worse, UV rays bounce off reflective surfaces such as glass, metal, and sidewalks.

UV rays reach some part of your body nearly every time you go outdoors, except at night. They can penetrate thin clothing and even affect places you wouldn't expect, like your scalp. These rays also enter through windows in buildings; if the interior of your home or office enjoys an abundance of natural light, chances are you're being exposed to significant UV rays even when you're indoors.

As we continue to unlock the powerful benefits of cannabinoids, studies are showing CBD combats the damage caused by UV rays.[55] Our immune and endocannabinoid systems are in hyper-drive to limit and repair damage while expediting new skin cell growth. Any kinks or gaps in our armor could prove debilitating or worse. That's why it's essential to educate ourselves, take care of our skin, and seek guidance from healthcare professionals.

UV Rating

Looking out the window will not tell you how intense the UV rays are that day. Wouldn't it be great if there was a device like a thermometer that registers the UV exposure in real time? Guess what, there is! You can consult the UV Index online, and it shows ratings in various areas on a

55. Leinow and Birnbaum, *CBD: A Patient's Guide*, 83–84.

map from a scale of low to high exposure. The National Weather Service developed the tool in conjunction with the Environmental Protection Agency based on guidelines established by the World Health Organization. The scale runs from low risk to high, from 0 to 11 plus, and each number has a recommendation regarding exposure times and sun protection. There's even a downloadable phone app to access the UV Index. See the Resources section at the end of the book for a link.

UV rays are responsible for different types of damage, but the biggest concerns are aging and cancer. The rays cause up to 80 percent of skin aging. Skin cancers are the most devastating form of skin aging, and melanoma is the most aggressive and deadly skin cancer.

If those rays are in sunlight, how do you avoid them? The answer is, you don't. You have to block them. Some dermatologists and medical professionals recommend using sunscreen or sunblock every day. When I suffered from my skin condition, I developed a hypersensitivity to sunlight and got in the habit of applying a "full-spectrum" UVA- and UVB-blocking product after my shower every morning. I think that's actually a good routine for everyone. The good news is that these products have come a long way in the last decade. Many are now dry to the touch and can be applied in the morning like moisturizer right after your shower. Use an organic product that contains CBD combined with non-micronized zinc oxide and you'll be helping repair cellular damage in your skin while you protect from UV rays.

Sun Protection

Sunblock and sunscreen are an absolute must for skin protection. Traditionally, sunblock was any product that created a physical barrier (such as zinc oxide or titanium oxide) against UV rays, while sunscreen worked by way of a chemical "screen" that absorbed and minimalized UV rays rather than blocking them altogether. Sunscreen generally works best on UVA rays, while sunblock is more effective on UVB rays.

These days, the difference is largely irrelevant. Most major brands offer "full-spectrum" products meant to block out both types of UV rays. Increasingly, people just turn to the SPF rating on a product to guide them in their choice. But there is also a lot of misunderstanding around the term "SPF." SPF is an acronym for "sun protection factor." Frankly, I agree with the many dermatologists pushing for an entirely new system of sunblock classification. (See pages 206–210 for a complete explanation of SPF and sun protection formulas.) Most consumers think that 30 SPF offers twice the protection of 15 SPF sunblock. It doesn't. It's only meant to last longer. Unfortunately, the issue is more complex than a single number on a label.

For instance, many sun-protection lotions are meant to be applied at least thirty minutes before sun exposure and reapplied regularly thereafter—more frequently if you're being active, sweating, or in and out of water. As with all skincare products, checking labels—including application instructions and precautions—is key.

As an aside, the sun isn't the only source of UV rays many people encounter. Tanning salons and tanning beds do just as much damage to your skin. In fact, a tan is actually the sign of your melanin's response to damage and a clear symptom that you've received too much UV exposure. Overexposure to UV rays can cause a host of other problems as well, including premature skin aging, excess wrinkling, a leathery texture, and precancerous changes. I strongly urge all my patients and anyone reading this book to completely avoid artificial tanning. In my mind, it's akin to purposely exposing yourself to radioactive waste in an effort to play Russian roulette with cancer. An attractive salon tan is simply not worth the potential price you'll pay.

History and Physiology

We are all uniquely defined by our skin type, life experiences, genes, and even our stage of life. That's why it's essential when considering your skin health to pay attention to factors that are important but perhaps less obvious. These factors help guide you when it comes to using CBD and cannabinoids for skin health.

For instance, family history can play a big part in your susceptibility to different types and severities of skin conditions. If a close relative has been afflicted with a serious skin condition, it's worth asking your dermatologist about whether the condition is hereditary. Many skin cancers, for example, have a genetic component. If one of your parents has been afflicted with a skin cancer, it's wise to start professional, full-body skin scans in your twenties.

Hormones also play a big part in many common skin diseases. Hormones are your body's messengers, and each one matches receptors in specific cells. When the balance of hormones is disrupted, it causes problems. This is most common during life changes. Teenage acne, for instance, is often the result of, or made worse by, the rush of hormones associated with puberty. Of course, hormones can also be put out of balance during less profound times of change, such as the menstrual cycle.

Chloasma is a hormonal reaction so common with pregnant women it's known as "the mask of pregnancy." The condition is characterized by a darkened area of skin, often around the mouth or on the face.

Menopausal women frequently experience a range of skin conditions. Signs can be modest, such as an increase in the fine lines around the eyes and mouth. Or, as estrogen and progesterone diminish and stop spurring glands to produce oil, menopausal skin may become irritatingly dry. Hot flashes create a flushed appearance. Severe conditions associated with menopause can even lead to slow, inefficient wound healing.

Other disorders and diseases can have a distinct hormonal element that affects skin health. For instance, hypothyroidism is a condition in which the thyroid does not produce enough thyroid hormone. Undiagnosed, the condition can cause scaly, thick, rough skin called *myxedema*.

The point is, always take a moment to consider context, your life stage, and possible health conditions or disorders when you notice any new skin symptom. I would recommend that women going through menopause, including peri- and post-menopause, consider microdosing with a CBD tincture. You'll be starting with 2 mg of CBD and slowly increasing the amount until you notice some relief from your symptoms. For other, sex-related issues, many women find relief with vaginal suppositories containing CBD. This is a highly efficient delivery system.

Lifestyle Factors

Your skin reflects the choices you make in life. Are you a smoker? If so, you can expect premature skin aging, a dull and unhealthy skin tone (the result of consistently depriving skin of essential oxygen and nutrients), unattractive loose sections of skin such as bags under the eyes, and increased wrinkling due to loss of elasticity. Some studies point to smoking contributing to and exacerbating psoriasis.[56] And, of course, smoking increases the risk of cancer, including skin cancers. The decreased blood flow that results from a regular smoking habit also inhibits wound healing. Quitting smoking is one of the best steps you can take to improve skin health and your appearance.

Sleep is also crucial for healthy skin, and CBD may aid in getting sound sleep. Tinctures of CBD, pure or in combination with other cannabinoids, have been shown to help calm the body and help with a good night's sleep. I would start with 10 mg of pure CBD and work your way to 20 mg if you don't experience the desired effect. A bad night's sleep cheats the body out of valuable cellular repair time. During sleep, blood flow increases to the extremities, spurring oxygenation of the skin and subsequently kicking repair mechanisms into high gear. That blood flow also removes waste debris and excess fluid, eliminating the puffiness you might notice after a bad night's sleep.

Similarly, the stress that may cause a lack of sleep contributes to skin damage and skin diseases. A vicious cycle

56. Arathi R. Setty, Gary Curhan, and Hyon K.Choi, "Smoking and the Risk of Psoriasis in Women: Nurses' Health Study II," *The American Journal of Medicine* 120, no. 11 (November 2007): 953–59, https://doi.org/10.1016/j.amjmed.2007.06.020.

can occur if you regularly sleep poorly. Among other effects, sleep deprivation elevates levels of the stress you experience. Stress increases the amount of adrenaline and cortisol in your system, which can increase blood sugar, accelerating inflammatory reactions and depressing immune-system response. This translates to slower wound healing and outbreaks or exacerbation of conditions such as eczema and acne. All that, in turn, can be an impediment to deep, restful sleep. And so on. Ongoing sleep deprivation can even contribute to premature skin aging and weight gain. Long-term chronic stress has even been found to increase the risk of skin cancer in lab mice and has proven to accelerate skin cell aging.

Eating for Skin Health

Another practice of mine with critically complex patients is to establish a good nutritional plan to help the patient endure and heal from illness and injury. The building blocks for health and wellness are largely synthesized from our liver, which is reliant on our gut health. CBD and cannabinoids have been shown to have great influence on gut health, digestion, and absorption of nutrients. This, in turn, helps the body maintain proper protein levels. Cannabinoids also boost the body's ability to fight damage from free radicals in our diet.

Nutrition also plays a key role in skin health. I urge my patients not to think about one food or another as the key to health—for skin or any other part of the body. Yes, certain foods may trigger outbreaks of a condition such as rosacea. In general, though, overall diet is more important than any one particular food or drink. There is no skin superfood that, taken alone, will suddenly boost skin health or reverse damage to the skin.

A diet high in processed foods, and especially one rich in refined carbohydrates and refined sugar, is going to have a negative impact on your skin, just as it will on all your organs. The more you eat these foods, the more your body develops insulin resistance. Insulin is the gate-keeper that allows blood sugar to enter cells. Resistance means that sugar builds up in the bloodstream, causing potentially massive damage to cells throughout the body, including in the skin. That damage can translate to pre-mature aging of the skin as well as an increased risk of skin diseases. There are also ancillary effects. Increased insulin resistance is linked to *acanthosis nigricans*, a con-dition marked by dark patches of velvety skin in areas where the skin creases or folds, such as armpits or under breasts. Out-of-control insulin resistance will inevitably lead to diabetes.

Weight gain is also related to maintaining an unhealthy diet (among many other factors, including genetic and hormonal predispositions). The physical stress and strain of carrying a lot of extra weight leads to vascular problems that show in the skin, such as spider and varicose veins.

On the other hand, any diet rich in antioxidants and omega-3 and omega-6 fatty acids will improve skin health. A diet weighted toward natural whole foods and vegetables will flood your system with essential vitamins and supplements, many of which improve skin health and appearance.

If you want to treat your skin to the best possible nutrition, focus on foods rich in omega-6 fatty acids. Do your skin a favor by regularly substituting cold-water fish, especially wild salmon, for meat. Look to integrate seeds and nuts as much as possible into your diet. Walnuts and sunflower seeds are particularly good, and great snack foods to replace an afternoon candy bar. Although a diet rich in vegetables and fresh fruits is always a good idea, I would also strongly recommend including foods most likely to contain beneficial fats—for example, avocados. I'm especially fond of broccoli, carrots, and kale for both their range of nutrients and cancer-fighting properties. Keep in mind that it's wise to eat these foods in both cooked and uncooked forms. Generally, the less you cook a vegetable, the more nutrients are preserved.

One quick aside here about supplements and vitamins. Your nutritional picture is a complicated one, and no one nutrient is a cure-all. A good diet, along with exercise and stress-reducing practices, is your first line of defense against skin or other health conditions. We are all susceptible to marketing and advertising messages over-selling the properties of one nutritional aid or another. But a handful of supplements will not make up for a det-rimental lifestyle, and I don't believe any one supplement will cure cancer. We also tend to think of supplements as completely benign, but it's actually quite possible to overdo any one supplement. For instance, excessively high amounts of vitamin A can cause liver damage. Whatever supplements you are thinking of adding into your diet, I'd strongly recommend that you consult with your doctor first. And read the supplement labels closely before using, just as you would with a drug.

Of course, not everything we ingest is eaten. Alcohol can be just as powerful a factor in skin health as junk food. Regular heavy drinking dehydrates the body, includ-ing the skin. More importantly, it causes inflammation throughout your system, the effects of which can last for days and may be cumulative. Although this can lead to an exacerbation of existing skin disease and can contribute to the onset of new conditions, it can also affect how your skin looks. Heavy drinking can leave skin looking dull with enlarged pores, sagging, areas of discoloration, and fine lines. Because alcohol dilates tiny blood vessels near the surface of the skin, long-term alcohol abuse can lead those vessels to burst. This is apparent where the skin is thinnest, such as the nose. This explains the characteristic "drinker's nose" and the unhealthy red skin tint in alcoholics. Drinking can also cause a domino effect because it disrupts sleep, leading to other problems.

On a related note, prescription and recreational drugs can have a profound effect on the skin. For instance, sulfur medications and certain types of antibiotics can increase photosensitivity. Anti-hypertensive medications, such as calcium channel blockers (*diltiazem*) and diuretic hydrochlorothiazide (HCTZ), are well known to cause local and systemic hyper-pigmented skin rashes with intense itching. Always check the list of side effects for any drug your doctor prescribes. If you are concerned about ill effects to your skin, ask your physician to prescribe an alternative. Illicit drugs can quickly cause serious and even irreversible skin damage and—it should go without saying—they should always be avoided.

Obviously, there is more than meets the eye when it comes to your skin. That's why I strongly recommend anyone highly susceptible to sunburns and individuals over the age of thirty-five find a reputable dermatologist and schedule regular yearly consultations, including a cancer skin scan. Melanoma is one of the deadliest cancers, and because sun exposure is so innocuous, you may not be aware of any problem or symptom before it's late in the game. A good dermatologist can also offer advice on how to head off or reverse skin aging, wrinkling, and other signs of wear and tear.

CBD offers a range of benefits that can help you keep your skin healthy as well as combat a variety of skin diseases and conditions. This cannabinoid affects not only the symptoms you may be experiencing but also the underlying conditions causing those symptoms. With an understanding of the skin's structure and functions (discussed in Chapter 6), it's time to take a deeper dive into exactly how CBD can be used to improve skin health.

8 · CBD FOR SKIN HEALTH AND DISEASE PREVENTION

YOUR SKIN IS YOUR body's force field, forming a nearly impregnable shield against major infections, illnesses, injuries, and accelerated aging. It plays an active role in maintaining core body temperature and is a window into your health; certain changes in the integrity of your skin signal the need for medical attention concerning what may be developing inside.

Those signs are why, before we get further into the skin-health potential of CBD, I want to emphasize the importance of working with an internist, a certified physician cannabis specialist, or both. Many patients I treat are so sick that skincare is the least of their medical concerns. But skin is perhaps the most blatant barometer of your general health. Having trouble sleeping? Chances are you have "bags" under your eyes. These are actually blood pooling under the thin skin beneath your eyes, causing puffiness. Imagine that clusters of waxy bumps suddenly show up on your shoulder. Those could be signs of heart disease. Diagonal earlobe creases, otherwise known as "Frank's sign," are associated with high cholesterol, coronary heart disease, and premature risk for stroke. Rashes, sores, ulcers, and discolorations can all be indicators of underlying disease, often the very first we notice. The point is, skin is incredibly complex. And let's face it, there's a lot of your skin you can't even see. Therefore, it is important to regularly consult with a medical professional and have your skin scanned on a regular basis for early indicators of underlying conditions.

As we have discussed in Chapter 3, the network of receptors, in tandem with endocannabinoids and regulatory enzymes, form your natural endocannabinoid system, or ECS. This system's sole purpose is to maintain harmony and to "right size" any changes or insults to our body. The skin's ECS echoes the plant-based phytocannabinoid system, and that's why plant-derived CBD provides such positive benefits for your skin. CBD affects receptors, which then set off a chain reaction that restores balance and maintains overall health.

A key take-home concept is that our natural ECS regulates normal skin-cell turnover or programmed death.

As skin cells die, they're replaced by new, more radiant, plumper cells. A disturbance in this natural lifecycle results in disease and accelerated aging. This manifests on our skin as wrinkles, patches, dermatitis, moles, and tumors. When you go to the makeup counter at your favorite department store and see "anti-aging" on the labels of all those creams and lotions, that's part of what they're talking about: efficient cell regeneration through timely cell death and replacement. It's why anti-aging is prominent among the many benefits that are touted by CBD proponents. I've experienced this myself. After I started regularly using a CBD formula for my runaway skin rash, people I met at parties, other events, and at work consistently thought I was younger than I am—usually by five years or more.

Cell "death" sounds a little gruesome, but it's a positive thing. It's key to fighting cancer. Cancer is—at its root— cells that have gone haywire and don't die as they should. When it comes to skin, these cells proliferate to form hyper-pigmented and irregularly shaped spots, moles, or scaly rashes. Their reproduction may also result in tumor growth or abnormal scarring. No surprise that among the research studies in progress are many focusing on CBD's potential for preventing, and even serving as one component in, treating cancers, including melanoma.

So how does CBD maintain proper skin health? The short answer is through its powerful anti-inflammatory and antioxidant properties. By stimulating certain CBD receptors on the skin, inflammation can be prevented or significantly limited, allowing for robust skin health and healing.

In ancient India, a thick layer of cannabis plant powder was applied to treat infected and diseased skin, similar to how we in the West use pure aloe or aloe creams and lotions for skin healing. I am especially excited at the possibility that CBD can be used to accelerate skin healing. This hits home for me because I've treated thousands of patients suffering from complicated traumatic surgical and non-surgical wounds and pressure ulcers. It is essential to keep the wounds clear of inflammation and infection. Our current options are to use a scalpel to remove overlying dead tissue or debris, or to use powerful chemicals with enzymes that will, at a much slower pace, chew away the necrotic tissue. Either method tends to be very painful and strong pre- and post-treatment painkillers are standard.

Now let's talk about antioxidants. You've seen that term a lot if you've ever shopped for skincare products. You've probably also seen it in advertising for shampoo and even food. It's a natural marketing hook because antioxidants fight free radicals. Free radicals are oxygen atoms that split off a molecule, leaving them with a single, highly charged electron. These charged electrons wreak great havoc and damage throughout our bodies in their quest for stabilization by partnering with another electron. In this world, two electrons are safer than one. Free radicals strip electrons from healthy proteins, DNA, and cell membranes, and they cause oxidation. Oxidation is uniformly destructive, as we can see with rust on machine parts or browning of cut fruits. That's oxidation at work and, as those examples illustrate, it can work fast and spread quickly. In the human body, oxidation causes diseases including cancer and coronary heart disease and will accelerate skin aging. All you really need to know at the end of the day is that free radicals and the oxidation they cause are bad. Antioxidants are good. They clean up free radicals, removing them from your system.

Some of the most common and powerful antioxidants that find their way into consumer products are vitamins E, C, A, and the compound resveratrol that is found in blueberries, raspberries, grapes, and peanuts. Polyphenol (certain plant-based micronutrients) antioxidants in green tea can have a beneficial impact in helping prevent certain skin cancers and protecting against sun UV ray damage. Regulatory enzymes in our bodies synthesize and break down our natural cannabinoids to head off some of the damage from smoking, UV ray exposure, and other environmental assaults. CBD, in combination with other plant-based cannabinoids, beats them all for pure antioxidant oomph. Hemp oil is also a wonderful source of omega-3 and omega-6 fatty acids, compounds that help the skin retain moisture and maintain cell suppleness—two aspects of fighting skin aging.

Beyond supplementing a rich and varied diet, CBD can serve just as important of a role in terms of personal relief. If you've ever suffered through an outbreak of dermatitis or a similar condition, you'll know just how much the itching and pain burrow into your mind and can monopolize your concentration.

Your skin also has the greatest matrix of nerve endings. Our nervous system is just waiting to report to the brain any change involving the skin, usually translating that change to some uncomfortable feeling such as itching, pain, or burning. That's great when we bump against something hot or are exposed to external stimuli that we can get away from. But when the nerves send those messages constantly in response to skin problems, they're just amplifying our pain and suffering. Furthermore, our inability to tolerate pain has resulted in our culture's unhealthy dependency on painkillers such as opioids and their subsequent abuse. Although our ancestors have used it as a safe, effective painkiller for thousands of years, we are just starting to scratch the surface of medical cannabis for pain management. In a related trend, many studies have shown real promise and success for using CBD to slowly detox from, and eventually be free of, opioid addiction (and other addictions as well, such as alcoholism).[57]

I know myself that itching and pain can be the worst parts of a skin condition. Symptoms like those are relayed by "transient receptor potential vanilloid" channels (TRPV1) that play vital roles as CBD receptors. Otherwise known as capsaicin receptors, TRP receptors modulate a whole host of pain, itch, and temperature sensations. They also manage inflammation, hair follicles, sebaceous glands, and strive for overall skin homeostasis or harmony.

These receptors are as numerous as CB1 and CB2 receptors are throughout your body—including your skin. In addition to influencing CBD receptors and blocking the enzymes that break down anandamide, CBD binds directly to TRPs. This binding is even more powerful in quelling sensations of pain and itching. Stopping that nagging irritation is important to prevent patients from further inflaming a skin problem or even spreading infection. The mechanism of CBD also works on more

_____

57. Reiman, Welty, and Solomon, "Cannabis as a Substitute," 160–66, https://doi.org/10.1089/can.2017.0012; Daniel J. Liput, et al., "Transdermal Delivery of Cannabidiol Attenuates Binge Alcohol-Induced Neurodegeneration in a Rodent Model of an Alcohol Use Disorder," *Pharmacology Biochemistry and Behavior* 111 (October 2013): 120–27, https://doi.org/10.1016/j.pbb.2013.08.013.

common forms of skin pain caused by run-of-the-mill conditions like sunburn, scrapes, bug bites, and similar small wounds.

Many skin conditions stem from the over- or under-production of oil from your pores and glands. An imbalance can even be detrimental to your overall health. Pores can get plugged with skin debris mixed with oil, bacteria, viruses, or fungi. Your body's response to prevent trauma and quickly restore balance relies heavily on the production and regulation of anandamide, which is almost chemically identical to CBD and THC. All three of these compounds bind and stimulate our natural cannabinoid and TRP receptors, helping the skin and body heal, promoting well-being, and maintaining good health. Anandamide can force either an increase or decrease of oil production, signaling our brain to stimulate anti-inflammatory defenses deep in our skin layers.

Anandamide is a fatty acid, a "lipid neurotransmitter" produced by the brain. It binds to the same receptors used by THC to get people high. Anandamide plays a powerful role in your mental state and sense of well-being, similar to endorphins, those powerful hormones produced in the body that create a "runner's high."[58]

Specific Diseases CBD Can Impact

Among the skin conditions that follow are many that can't currently be cured, and this list is not meant to suggest that CBD can cure skin conditions. One of the common denominators underlying all skin diseases is the cascade of events that result in various degrees of inflammation. Most plans of treatment center on reducing, eliminating, and ultimately preventing the cycle of injury and inflammation. CBD and other cannabinoids can powerfully and organically aid in that and play a part in your quest for well-being and freedom from pain and suffering.

Acne

For sufferers, acne can be frustrating and embarrassing. Bad outbreaks can even leave permanent scarring, with lifelong psychological impact on self-esteem. The condition can lead to anxiety, depression, and even thoughts of suicide. This one skin condition affects tens of millions of people who spend billions of dollars to combat it—much

---

58. Johannes Fuss, et al., "A Runner's High Depends On Cannabinoid Receptors In Mice," *Proceedings of the National Academy of Sciences of the United States of America* 112, no. 42 (October 2015): 13105–108, https://doi.org/10.1073/pnas.1514996112.

of that, unsuccessfully. Even worse, treatment comes with risks of side effects and complications from prescription antibiotics, benzoyl peroxide, salicylic acid, or Isotretinoin (Accutane). In fact, Accutane has been linked to fetal death during pregnancy.

The problem is that acne's cause is not completely understood. It represents a perfect storm of hormonal imbalance, excess oil production, and other less tangible factors such as stress, genetics, or eating foods rich in processed sugar—a strongly inflammatory ingredient. This much we know: The visible outbreak is caused by oil, skin debris, and bacteria trapped at the base of hair follicles. That mixture results in unsightly pimples and blackheads that can easily lead to further infection. Ongoing inflammation causes oxidative stress that can be unhealthy over time.[59] The reverse is also true: oxidative stress causes inflammation. A goal in treating any condition like acne is to curtail this "domino effect."

Preliminary research has shown that oral CBD can reduce the frequency and severity of acne outbreaks.

59. Anna Machowska, et al., "Therapeutics Targeting Persistent Inflammation in Chronic Kidney Disease," *Translational Research* 167, no. 1 (January 2016): 204–13, https://doi.org/10.1016/j. trsl.2015.06.012; Bruce B. Duncan, et al., "Low-Grade Systemic Inflammation and the Development of Type 2 Diabetes," *Diabetes* 52, no. 7 (July 2003): 1799–805, https://doi.org/10.2337 /diabetes.52.7.1799.

As described in a 2014 study published in the *Journal of Clinical Investigation*, CBD influences skin cells to produce less oil, and it reduces the specific inflammation that exacerbates acne.[60] Although the exact mechanisms by which CBD combats acne are still being investigated, the cannabinoid has a significant impact on the critical factors that make acne worse. The first is that CBD promotes a balanced, healthy skin ECS. Not only does it play a part in regulating cell growth, it also inhibits excessive oil production from hair follicles and sebaceous glands. CBD also undercuts the severity of any acne attack by reducing inflammation and isolating pimples to limit spread of bacteria. Furthermore, CBD reduces pain, sensations of itching, and the consequent incessant need to scratch. That is critical to preventing further skin trauma and spread of infection.

CBD for acne is usually delivered topically. A topical formulation doesn't need to go especially deep or penetrate the skin-blood barrier to have an effect on the oil production and inflammation typical of an acne outbreak. I would advise using a product formulated for skin conditions rather than simply a beauty cream, because the

---

60. Oláh, et al., "Cannabidiol Exerts Sebostatic and Antiinflammatory Effects on Human Sebocytes," *Journal of Clinical Investigation* 124, no. 9 (September 2014): 3713–24, https://doi.org/10.1172/JCI64628.

product is more likely to contain a substantial amount of CBD per application. It is also important that you investigate the product you're considering to make sure you're getting the quality and amount of CBD advertised.

For regular acne outbreaks, I'd suggest supplementing topical applications with daily oral doses of CBD. You can take capsules, but I prefer tinctures as sublingual drops because the dose is likelier to be maintained at the strength you've chosen. For oral doses, start with 20 mgs divided in twice-a-day doses and increase by 5 mg every five to seven days until you've noticeably impacted the frequency and severity of any outbreaks. Topical applications can be integrated as part of a daily skincare regimen; I would choose a formula with 100 mgs per 4 ounces or higher. Tap the CBD solution lightly around the pus-filled bumps to isolate infection, treat inflammation, and decrease any associated urge to scratch. Because acne can be so persistent, it's essential that you work with a CBD-knowledgeable dermatologist or physician in coming up with your treatment. He or she will be able to give specific instructions on the use of any CBD cream, ointment, or serum in conjunction with any medical preparations the doctor might prescribe for the condition.

Generally, CBD topical formulations are best applied after a routine skin cleansing. If you're using any topical product containing retinol, I would suggest applying that product first, waiting fifteen to twenty minutes, and then applying the CBD preparation. Remember to always gently blot your skin dry to avoid irritation or further trauma to inflamed skin. Test a small area before using a wider daily application to observe any reactions. If, after about two weeks, you are tolerating the dose and want a greater effect, consider a topical oil with a 5:1 ratio of CBD to THC (assuming THC is legal in your state). This can be especially effective on moderate to severe acne.

One side note here. There are many different strains of hemp from which CBD is extracted. How well a given product works for you may depend on the plant's chemotypes. Don't be afraid to change to a CBD lotion or oil from a different strain of plant. Similarly, controlling dosage in topical applications is difficult, and you can't always account for other additives in a cream or lotion.

Itching is mediated by our brain and spinal cord from surface nerve stimulation. The act of scratching may temporarily relieve symptoms by interfering with these signals to the brain. However, the mechanical act of scratching actually disrupts local healing in the layers of our skin and can cause inflammation. This creates a vicious cycle. If itching has become a major issue in your acne breakouts, consult your physician about treatment options.

A medical colleague of mine has struggled with acne throughout most of his life and has found great relief with

CBD. His acne breakouts have been greatly reduced since using topical CBD.

Eczema

Most common in childhood, eczema can and often does afflict adults. Eczema appears as red, itchy, and scaly skin patches. It is caused by an allergic reaction to an inhaled or ingested antigen, such as dust mites, grass, pet dander, or certain foods—most commonly peanuts. Our immune system goes into a frenzy trying to protect us, yet on the surface this fight presents as traumatized and often painful skin. Hypersensitive responses are mostly due to inherited gene mutations that lead to a lifelong susceptibility.

A young adult daughter of a nurse who used to work at my hospital has been battling episodes of eczema. She began applying topical CBD to affected areas on the back of her hands and neck. Within one week she was excited to tell me that her rash was improving. The purplish-red discoloration and her need to scratch off the flaky dead skin had significantly decreased. CBD is now a tool in her toolbox in conjunction with minimizing her exposure to allergens.

In another case, a mother I met showed me photos of her five-year-old son's eczema-type rash. The rash ranged from the knees to the shins on both of his legs. The poor child was at wit's end from pain and itchiness, and his pediatrician was reportedly unable to offer any solutions.

The mother applied a mild CBD balm, and by the next day, the rash was mostly gone. Unfortunately, there was still some itching, but she appreciated that he had some level of relief.

There are several types of eczema that share the symptomatic rash and relentless itching. They are grouped under the general term "dermatitis."

Atopic dermatitis afflicts hay fever and allergy sufferers and is thought to be part of more general allergic reactions. *Contact dermatitis* is, as the name implies, a reaction to an external irritant such as chemicals in body care products, latex, or poison oak. *Seborrheic dermatitis* is characterized by distinctively scaly, itchy skin, often breaking out on the scalp and neck. *Dyshidrotic eczema* includes sometimes-painful, fluid-filled blisters, and *nummular eczema* produces circular areas of irritated skin. *Stasis dermatitis* includes swelling of the ankles and feet.

Breaking the vicious cycle of itching and scratching is crucial to healing any outbreak of eczema. Incessant itching and scratching only leads to increased pain, misery, and the risk for more serious infections. Scratching falsely provides us a sense of relief.

Before we talk treatments, it's important to understand that the underlying state allowing eczema to manifest is some combination of autoimmunity and exposure to an allergen. Despite the treatments I suggest below, the first order of business if you are afflicted by chronic eczema is to find out what is triggering the outbreaks and isolate the allergen so you can take steps to avoid it in the future. That means a consultation with a reputable allergist and dermatologist—and possibly undergoing both blood and skin patch testing. Here again, I recommend an integrative approach and working with a medical CBD specialist.

The key to breaking the negative loop in eczema is the action of "mast" cells. Mast cells release histamines when triggered, and those histamines set off the terrible itching. CBD appears to suppress the action of mast cells, alleviating much of the itching. CBD's anti-inflammatory properties also help lessen the severity of any eczema outbreak.

The ideal CBD delivery method for an eczema flare-up is a thick layer of topical cream or ointment once or twice a day. This should contain pure CBD from a verified source in a dose close to 10 to 20 mg per application. After four to five days, the dose may be doubled as tolerated. If symptoms persist after two weeks, continue with an application of the same dose twice a day. It may be necessary to change from pure isolated CBD to full-spectrum or switch to CBD from a different source or plant if symptoms persist (as long as you do not exhibit intolerance to the CBD itself).

Research indicates that eczema, especially in severe cases, is responsive to the entourage effect of combining cannabinoids in a treatment.[61] If it's legal in your state, I recommend using a topical product with CBD and THC in a ratio of 5:1 to start. I highly recommend working with a medical CBD expert and your primary care physician to tailor the best course of action to your case and to avoid any side effects due to other health conditions. You should also consult a medical professional to avoid any drug interactions with prescription medications.

Depending on the manufacturer, CBD creams for skincare can contain impurities or ingredients that may actually irritate the skin and exacerbate eczema. That's why it's crucial to buy a formula from a reputable source and get a list of suspect ingredients from your allergist. Any cream, ointment, or salve meant for joint pain will likely contain ingredients that will worsen eczema. Buying an organic, aloe-based cream is a good idea. If you're applying CBD oil in any formula, make sure it is pure and from a reputable manufacturer.

---

61. Aurelia Tubaro, et al., "Comparative Topical Anti-inflammatory Activity of Cannabinoids and Cannabivarins," *Fitoterapia* 81, no. 7 (October 2010): 816–19, https://doi.org/10.1016/j. fitote.2010.04.009; Hyun Jong Kim, et al., "Topical Cannabinoid Receptor 1 Agonist Attenuates the Cutaneous Inflammatory Responses in Oxazolone-Induced Atopic Dermatitis Model," *International Journal of Dermatology* 54, no. 10 (October 2015): 401–08, https://doi.org/10.1111/ijd.12841.

Melanoma

Cancer is the scariest of all diseases, and skin cancer is no less so. Cancer develops when the normal cells are genetically altered and grow unchecked into nodules and tumors. These cells obtain their fuel from hijacking normal blood flow and nutrients from healthy tissue and organs, resulting in catastrophic illness if not caught early. Any potential tool in the fight against cancer raises a lot of interest in the medical community. That's why CBD has grabbed the attention of many cancer researchers.

Early detection of precancerous or suspicious skin lesions is essential to preventing the onset of cancer, or treating it in its earliest, weakest stages. Unfortunately, melanoma has the distinction of being one of the most aggressive, invasive, and potentially fatal cancers. Other skin cancers, such as basal cell carcinoma and squamous cell carcinoma, are far less likely to be fatal.

The public has been well educated on the benefits of protecting skin from sunlight UV ray exposure and avoiding tanning booths. But exposure to unusually high levels of radiation from sources such as X-rays, and changes in our immune system from exposure to allergens and infections that weaken the skin's structure, also lead to higher risk of skin cancer. Furthermore, melanoma can present on the soles of your feet, on the scalp, behind the ears, or even in the mouth. I highly recommend developing a routine to scan and photograph any changes in your skin. Make these a part of your regular health checkups and discuss them with your doctor.

CBD was first used to alleviate the side effects of more traditional cancer treatments. For instance, patients have turned to CBD capsules, edibles, and vaping to lessen the nausea and loss of appetite so common with chemotherapy. Research shows that CBD can also have a positive impact on the anxiety and pure mental stress that comes from dealing with a life-threatening illness like cancer.[62]

As we learn more about the complex way CBD works, and how it complements so many wellness mechanisms the body uses to heal itself, its potential as a cancer fighter has become a fertile area for study. Preliminary research on how CBD may indirectly influence cell death points to the possibility that high-dose CBD could play a part in killing cancer cells—including melanoma. In fact, a 2018 study published in the *Journal of Surgical Research* found that CBD helped shrink melanoma tumors in lab mice.[63] It's a

---

62. Maria Morena, et al., "Neurobiological Interactions between Stress and the Endocannabinoid System," *Neuropsychopharmacology* 41, no. 1 (January 2016): 80–102, https://doi.org/10.1038/npp.2015.166.

63. Erika Simmerman, et al., "Cannabinoids as a Potential New and Novel Treatment for Melanoma: A Pilot Study in a Murine Model," *Journal of Surgical Research* 235 (March 2019): 210–15, https://doi.org/10.1016/j.jss.2018.08.055.

far cry from a human clinical trial, but it's a start and holds some promise for the future of melanoma treatment.

A caveat here. At this point in time, CBD should only be considered as a complement to conventional medical treatments for cancer. As with all potential health panaceas, social media and the internet at large host a proliferation of miracle stories. It's not hard to find anecdotes of someone curing their own cancer with CBD oil. I counsel restraint, caution, and skepticism when it comes to life-threatening diseases. I believe CBD may possibly be one of several components in preventing and fighting cancer, including melanoma. But I'm eager to see the results of further studies on how this powerful tool might be used in combatting the illness. I urge you to follow the studies underway using the National Institutes of Health website listed in the Resources section at the end of this book.

Regardless of whether you decide to integrate CBD into your daily skincare regimen, prevention and early detection remain among the best tools for fighting the onset or recurrence of melanoma.

Psoriasis

Simply put, psoriasis is a chronic skin condition characterized by rapid overproduction of skin cells. It appears as scaly red and silver patches that are extremely itchy and painful. Your skin cells' life cycle averages about a month.

Cells form in the deepest layer and eventually push to the top before naturally flaking off. With psoriasis, this cycle is grossly accelerated, taking only a few days. Psoriasis is often associated with, and may be an early indicator for, other autoimmune conditions such as diabetes, inflammatory bowel disease, and even skin cancers. Outbreaks have been linked to physical and mental stress and lifestyle factors such as smoking and overwork. Some combination of THC, CBD, CBN, and CBC can help fight psoriasis.

Plaque psoriasis is the most common type, presenting raised areas of angry, scaly skin lesions. The lesions are medically called "plaques," thus the name. Outbreaks range from mild to severe and can occur anywhere on the body. *Inverse psoriasis* is much rarer, occurring in the skin folds on the body—areas such as the armpits, groin, or under breasts. The affected areas are smoother than with other types of psoriasis but may still be sensitive and even painful. *Pustular psoriasis* is, as the name implies, marked by the formation of pus-filled blisters. The condition can occur quickly and may be mistaken for a symptom of another disease because it is often accompanied by fever, chills, and even diarrhea. *Psoriatic arthritis* is a combination of joint swelling and damage coupled with red, often painful scaly skin in the affected area.

Because psoriasis is linked to immune system dysfunction, sufferers should consider an ongoing course of oral

CBD oil in the range of 10 to 20 mg once or twice a day while self-monitoring for tolerance. Increase the dose every five days by 5 mg to a maximum of 100 mg until you notice a change in the psoriasis. That can be supplemented with the application of a CBD cream to treat outbreaks when and where they occur, which should alleviate some if not all of the itching.

Psoriatic arthritis is a bit different because of the involvement of joints. Consider the regular intake of CBD orally as described above but used in conjunction with a deep-tissue CBD ointment meant to penetrate below the skin for outbreaks. However, before considering any penetrating formula, consult your doctor. Always keep in mind that skin conditions can be a window to more underlying serious health issues.

CBD proved to be a great help to a niece of one of my nurses. She had small patches of painful and itchy psoriasis on her elbows. These patches were red and bumpy and had the characteristic whitish dead skin scales on the surface. Her niece applied CBD-based serum to the rash and immediately felt relief. The patches were not as rough, and the redness started to abate.

Rosacea

Rosacea is one of the most embarrassing skin disorders because it most often occurs on the face. It manifests in several different ways. *Vascular rosacea* is character-ized by red areas and enlarged, clearly visible blood ves-sels. *Ocular rosacea* causes red, angry skin and swelling around the eyes and eyelids. *Inflammatory rosacea* is one of the most dramatic and stress-inducing forms, leading to large areas of redness and swelling, including blister-ing and pustules. *Phymatous rosacea* presents the oddest symptoms in which skin not only reddens but also thick-ens with a bumpy texture, and the nose may increase in size.

Any outbreak of rosacea is made more debilitating by the fact that the skin becomes very sensitive. Without treatment, the condition can become much worse. Unlike many skin conditions that are, in one form or another, allergic responses, rosacea is thought to be an overreac-tion of the immune system. As such, it requires consulta-tion with a dermatologist who will likely prescribe reti-naldehyde, topical antibiotics, and steroids. Because all of these have serious potential side effects, CBD oil can be an excellent complement to treatment. Make sure to ask your medical professional specifically about potential CBD interaction with steroid medications.

The fatty acids (omega-6 and omega-3) and anti-inflammatory properties of CBD can have a significant effect on calming a rosacea outbreak. I would recommend using CBD oil directly on affected areas from a beginning dose of 1 to 2 mg per day during an outbreak. If you don't see improvement in three to four days, increase the dose by 1 mg every two days to a maximum of 6 mg, all the while checking for tolerance. Rosacea may also respond to regular ingestion of CBD capsules. Begin with lower doses to ensure your system has no problem with the CBD and work up to a standard dose of 10 to 15 mg of CBD taken two to three times a day. Increase that dose as needed every two weeks to lessen the severity and number of outbreaks up to a total dose of 100 mg a day. As I've said before, work with a health care professional to decide on your specific course of care.

Shingles

Shingles is caused by a strain of the herpes virus and is one of the most painful skin conditions a person can experience. Anyone who had chickenpox as a child is a potential victim. The rash is often excruciating to the touch and usually occurs only on one side of the body. In addition to the topical pain, sufferers may experience headaches and fluid-filled blisters. There are two components to a shingles outbreak: the characteristic rash that can be sensitive, uncomfortable, and unsightly—but that goes away within weeks—and the neuropathic pain that is produced by the damaged nerves under the rash. That pain, unfortunately, can last a lifetime, flaring up even in the absence of a rash.

The pain caused by shingles is unique. The virus attacks nerve cells, disabling them. That, in turn, means many painkillers are not effective against shingles, and some sufferers struggle to find any relief at all. Given that the condition often occurs in combination with a compromised immune system, this can be a truly debilitating skin disease.

Fortunately, CBD binds to nerve receptors not affected by the virus. Although a topical application will not immediately stop the pain, it will start to reduce it, along with diminishing the inflammation that accompanies the telltale rash. This is also a case where a combination of CBD with THC can be very effective. Start with a ratio of 1:1 and increase the CBD as necessary to achieve relief. The combination works well because CB1 receptors are concentrated in the brain, including the pain centers of the brain. THC stimulates the CB1 receptors directly while the CBD boosts anandamide levels. It's an excellent combination for diminishing neuropathic pain.

Medical professionals have found that oral, topical, and even tinctures have an impact on this disease. Because shingles is a serious condition and can be coupled with an even more harmful underlying condition, you should always consult a medical professional when you have an outbreak. In general, I would recommend a dose of 10 mg of CBD taken three times a day, increasing slowly to 20 mg three times a day over a period of two to three weeks as you verify that you're tolerating the dose. With an active rash, I recommend a direct application of 2 mg of CBD oil one to two times a day, ramping up every two days by 1 mg one to two times a day as necessary, to a maximum of 10 mg to diminish pain and inflammation.

Bacterial Skin Infections

The skin is susceptible to a number of infections. Most of these also have an immune system component and can be exacerbated by underlying conditions and diseases. Bolstering the immune system should be part of the strategy in treating any skin infection (and any major infection in the body, for that matter). Most skin infections can be traced to the bacteria *Streptococcus* or *Staphylococcus aureus*. You're more likely to be infected in an environment potentially rich with the bacteria, such as a hospital, day care center, or even in an Uber.

Folliculitis

This is an infection at the base of hair follicles. In early stages, this infection presents as red bumps or white heads around the infected follicles. It can progress in some cases to open sores that are slow to heal. Usually, folliculitis resolves by itself in a few days. All you need to do is keep the area clean and dry and stop any exacerbating practices such as shaving or hot tubbing (a common type of folliculitis is actually caused by bacteria that breeds readily in hot tubs and spa tubs). Although most outbreaks of folliculitis are brief and fairly easily taken care of, there are rarer, more serious cases. These include a form called *eosinophilic*, common in HIV and AIDS patients, and *gram-negative folliculitis*, which afflicts long-term antibiotic users. In general, seek medical attention for any incidence of folliculitis that doesn't heal and go away within a few days, or any that create open sores, pus-filled carbuncles or boils, or large areas of affected skin.

Both topical and oral CBD can be a valuable weapon in preventing and fighting these infections. However, it's important to understand that any infection of the skin is potentially serious. CBD alone is not a complete treatment for these types of infections. In some cases, your doctor will prescribe topical or oral antibiotics. If this occurs, make sure you ask if any CBD you regularly take will interfere with the effectiveness of the prescribed antibiotics.

Cellulitis

This is an insidious infection that can affect deep skin tissues and even underlying structures. Left untreated, it can move quickly through lymph nodes and the bloodstream to become a systemic infection that constitutes a medical emergency. The infection often afflicts the lower legs and arms and appears as redness and swelling and will usually be noticeably warm to the touch. (Less often, cellulitis occurs on the face or other areas of the body.) This condition can also create flu-like symptoms and red streaks emanating from the infected area. The good news is that if caught and treated early, most patients make a complete recovery with no lasting symptoms. Oral or sublingual CBD—especially in combination with other cannabinoids such as CBN and CBG—can be an effective treatment complement to antibiotics in fighting a cellulitis infection. Regardless, any time you suspect cellulitis, you should immediately consult a medical professional.

Just as cellulitis affects the deep tissue, *erysipelas* infects the epidermal layer, causing a highly-visible rash, often with a burning feeling that is responsible for erysipelas's other name: "St. Anthony's Fire." Anyone with a compromised immune system has an increased susceptibly to erysipelas and related infections. The infection is usually accompanied by a fever, chills, vomiting, fatigue, and a general feeling of being sick. Because the infection is closely tied to conditions in which the immune system is significantly comprised, erysipelas has the potential to become a serious medical condition. Active treatment by a medical specialist early is key because this infection can spread and can even—in severe cases—lead to tissue death. Here again, an oral form of CBD complemented with a range of other cannabinoids will not only help boost a deficient immune system, it may also play a role in fighting the infection itself. A topical CBD cream or ointment can be used to diminish the characteristic burning sensation.

9 · SIDE EFFECTS, ALLERGIES, AND DRUG INTERACTIONS

ANY TIME YOU'RE CONSIDERING slathering something all over your skin or ingesting supplement capsules, you should take potential side effects into account. Compared to almost anything else you can put on your skin, CBD oil has incredibly negligible downsides. A topical application may result in skin warmth and redness, which will self-resolve within minutes to several hours. Ultimately, if side effects are bothering you, stop using the CBD. The side effects will disappear completely within a day or two.

Very rare serious side effects have been seen in patients using extremely high oral dosages of CBD for diseases such as epilepsy. Any patient with a potentially life-threatening illness should always consult a medical professional before incorporating CBD into a daily regimen.

Cannabis Hyperemesis Syndrome

Cannabis hyperemesis syndrome is a rare but well-reported condition of recurrent and persistent nausea, severe vomiting, cramping, and other abdominal pain. One of the stranger symptoms is the compulsion to take hot baths, which can alleviate symptoms to a degree. The symptoms can happen both episodically—as a one-time event—and cyclically depending on cannabis use. It's associated with years of daily high-dose cannabis use, and the majority of sufferers have been recreational marijuana users. But there have been some reports of CHS happening in more casual users. However, to keep things in perspective, the syndrome usually afflicts heavy users of THC. This can include patients dealing with severe or long-term pain who have turned to THC. Recreational users and patients who have procured cannabis illegally have historically been somewhat reluctant to come forward even to seek treatment.

The actual causes of the symptoms and why they affect one user and not another remains unknown. Some professionals theorize that excess and continual THC intake causes receptors in the brain to become desensitized, and those receptors then begin to react in the opposite fashion from their normal function. (Remember, normally THC and other cannabinoids help with nausea.)

Fortunately, the condition is fairly easy to resolve. The basic symptoms can be temporarily lessened or stopped with hot showers or baths, and the syndrome will be entirely stopped by simply discontinuing the use of cannabis. However, sufferers should consult with a medical professional as soon as possible, not only to diagnose the syndrome, but also to rule out other potential causes of the symptoms. A physician will also be able to identify and treat more severe complications such as a breakdown of muscle tissue (called *rhabdomyolysis*), kidney failure, or shock, which can result from the dehydration often caused by excessive vomiting.

Including a range of cannabinoids in any treatment regimen, such as raw plant precursors like CBDA, can be effective at heading off any possibility of CHS. But any time you regularly take cannabis, be mindful of side effects such as, but not limited to, morning discomfort and nausea. Consult a doctor as soon as they occur.

CBD allergic reactions are uncommon. They can range from mild cold-like symptoms to dangerous anaphylaxis. But in my experience and research, negative reactions are usually due to consuming edibles or vaping products from unreliable or untrustworthy sources. However, as I always tell my patients, everyone has their own unique chemistry.

Whenever you put something in or on your body, pay close attention to the effects. Even acetaminophen can cause side effects and adverse reactions. That's why my mantra is "start low and go slow." When in doubt, seek the counsel of a qualified medical cannabis doctor. Also investigate the source of any CBD in the products you buy and use.

Used topically on the skin, any side effects should be minimal; virtually no marked reaction has been noted in my experience or CBD skincare research done to this point. Even if you were to react to an application of a cream or ointment containing CBD, the reaction would diminish and clear up within a day or so by simply stopping your exposure to the product. The most significant side effects reported have been limited to drowsiness when ingesting CBD with THC. However, read labels carefully because other ingredients in over-the-counter preparations may cause more of a reaction.

The more important consideration is drug interactions between CBD and any prescription medications you may be using on your skin.

CBD and Drug Interactions

If you are taking prescription drugs, even topical drugs such as steroids, it's essential that you consult with your doctor before adding CBD to the mix. Even if you are taking the prescription drug for something unrelated to a skin condition, the CBD could still interfere with its intended effect—making the drug stronger or weaker. Many major drug categories require what's known as "first pass effect," activation and deactivation by P450 enzymes in the liver. Cannabinoids such as CBD and THC are no different. In a healthy liver, we have a certain number of these enzymes and they work at their own programmed speed, which varies based on our own unique genetic code.

But before you panic or throw out your CBD drops, understand that interactions are not common. They occur most often in cases where a patient is taking high-dose CBD, and the likelihood is increased when the CBD is an isolate (used alone without other cannabinoids or components of the plant). Also, because the liver is where a lot of interaction problems occur, vaped or sublingual delivery methods may lessen the chances of any interaction. This is one more reason to find a physician or healthcare provider certified in the use of medical cannabis and CBD.

Keep in mind that interactions with these is an extremely rare occurrence. Drug classes that may interact with CBD include:

- Antibiotics
- Anesthetics
- Antipsychotics

- Antidepressants
- Anti-epileptics
- Antihistamines
- Antiretrovirals
- Benzodiazepines
- Beta Blockers
- Blood Thinners
- Calcium Channel Blockers
- Proton Pump Inhibitors (PPIs, such as Prilosec)
- Statins
- Steroids (topical and oral)

A good rule of thumb is if the medication's directions state that it shouldn't be taken with grapefruit, the medication most likely should not be combined with CBD oil. CBD and the active ingredients in grapefruit interfere with drug metabolism in much the same way.

Contraindicated Conditions

Certain medical conditions may preclude the use of CBD or other cannabinoids. These include heart arrhythmia, COPD, kidney disease, and certain types of liver diseases. This is largely because most traditional medications are metabolized by the liver, kidney, or both. When our vital organs are weak due to disease, ingesting, inhaling, or even using CBD on the skin is not recommended. In these cases, the use of CBD can lead to more serious health complications. A medical physician must be consulted prior to any consideration for CBD or THC use.

CBD has also not been conclusively proven safe for pregnant women or women who are breastfeeding, and those individuals should consult their doctor before using even skin lotion containing CBD.

Obviously, CBD for skincare shouldn't be considered in isolation. Not only should you keep in mind any prescription drugs you might be taking, look at the skin holistically, as a part of the larger system of your body. Hydration, a balanced diet full of natural antioxidants, exercise, and taking steps to protect against harmful UV rays will always remain the foundation for skin health and a long and healthy life in general.

10 · CBD AND BEAUTY

BEAUTY EXPERTS HAVE LONG promoted the use of topical agents rich in vitamins C and E. That's understandable. Vitamin C stimulates collagen production, and vitamin E fights those nasty free radicals. And guess what? CBD is rich in both.

Remember CBD's anti-inflammatory properties? Well, that's not just a plus for treating skin disorders. The same effect reduces puffiness. The antioxidants in CBD oil, as well as the fatty acids that the cannabinoid contains, go far toward reducing age-related damage by nourishing new cell growth and effective turnover of dead cells. This process also strengthens our skin's fight against everyday assaults from UV rays, chemicals, and pollutants. Not only can a CBD formula help prevent damage, it can also reduce dull or weathered skin tones.

A Potent Beauty Product Ingredient

All of that makes CBD an excellent component in beauty products. Although even with something as benign as beauty products, I would still counsel starting "low" and going "slow" as you start using CBD-containing products. In makeup, CBD adds a super-conditioning agent to everything from blush to concealer to lip gloss. Replace the skin lotions and creams that you use regularly with versions infused with CBD and you'll be bathing your skin in essential fatty acids and a key inflammation fighter. Given the proliferation of beauty products containing CBD that are coming on the market right now, you could feasibly replace almost all your skincare and makeup products with versions containing CBD.

However, I would suggest using a more cautious approach. Start by introducing just one CBD product, such as a moisturizer, into your daily regimen. See if it has an effect and, if it doesn't, replace it with a similar product containing a greater amount of CBD. Once you're comfortable with that product, you can consider adding another one, such as a lipstick. Follow the same methodical process with that product and so on. This isn't just a matter of clinical caution; CBD is the big new thing and it is expensive to process. Reputable beauty companies are understandably charging a premium for many of these new products, so it also makes good financial sense to ensure that you're getting a noticeable result as a return on your beauty-product dollar.

CBD and Skin Aging

Fighting aging means pushing back against something that's destined to happen no matter what you do. Aging is a natural process. But many of the signs of aging, especially those reflected in the condition of your skin, are evidence of *how* you live rather than how long you've lived. And these days, modern health practices, the most contemporary beauty products, and other innovations mean older people are looking younger than ever—and they want to stay that way. Any strategy to combat the more visible indicators of aging starts with the low-hanging fruit of good general health practices. As effective as CBD and other skincare age-fighters might be, there's no substitute for an excellent diet, regular exercise, stress reduction, and a good night's sleep.

Beyond those lifestyle factors, it's essential to understand what's happening as you age if you're going to combat the effects aging has already taken on your skin. In a sense, getting older can be boiled down to losing what we'd like to keep and gaining what we'd prefer to avoid.

For instance, as we age, the body produces less collagen and elastin, reducing the elasticity and fullness in skin tissue. There is also a profound deterioration of the web that forms the underlying attachment holding the dermis in place and further protects the skin from physical injury. All this leads to increased sagging, wrinkling, irregular texture, and the other obvious external effects of aging.

As you get older, especially once you reach your forties, the epidermis noticeably thins. It contains less and less fat and fewer *ceramides*, the glue that binds the epidermal cells together. As the skin becomes thinner and drier, it is more prone to damage. When damage occurs, it shows more profoundly because the repair mechanisms are less efficient. The rate at which skin cells turn over slows as we age, sometimes dramatically. This can cause a dull complexion and a coarse skin texture.

The most noticeable damage from skin aging takes place in the extracellular matrix (ECM). As you'll recall from earlier in the book (Chapter 6), the ECM is the thickest part of the dermis, the sub-layer that keeps skin plump and youthful looking. Envision the ECM as the scaffold responsible for our skin's texture and shape and the collagen and elastin as its bricks and mortar. In the great balancing act of our health, the production of new collagen and elastin is matched by the dismantling and recycling of older components in the ECM. This process is enabled by enzymes known as *matrix metalloprotein-ases* (MMPs) that break down and remove sun-, injury-, or disease-damaged collagen and other waste products. But as we age, that give-and-take is thrown out of whack, and we produce less new collagen and elastin than the MMPs break down. That makes the entire ECM weaker and less stable. That change translates to sagging skin, enlarged pores, coarse skin texture, and irregular skin coloring.

Any anti-aging compound or product is intended to fight some or all of these factors by stopping or slowing the damage that causes and exacerbates them. They are supposed to do this by hydrating cells, spurring collagen production, reducing inflammation, and fighting destructive byproducts such as free radicals and MMPs. Before we get into the relative efficiency of different age fighters, though, let's drill down into the actual causes of skin aging.

Factors in Skin Aging

Although it is a natural process, aging and its effects on the skin are made worse and sped up by a number of internal and external factors. The worst culprit is sunlight. By many accounts, sun damage from UV rays contributes up to 90 percent of the obvious signs of skin aging.

When the rays penetrate the skin, they spur the creation of a particular type of free radical known as reactive oxygen species (ROS), an especially damaging version of an already destructive molecule. It's a double whammy because, ironically, the same UV rays diminish the number of free-radical-fighting antioxidants in each layer of skin. The result of ROS in your skin is what's known as "oxidative stress." That stress leads to skin laxity (looseness), overproduction of melanin (which creates skin discoloration and what are commonly called liver spots), spider veins, and visibly enlarged pores. UV rays also increase the concentration of MMPs, which further deteriorates the all-important ECM. That, in turn, makes all the signs of aging worse.

As bad as sunlight may be, all these negative effects are made incrementally worse by lifestyle choices such as smoking and seemingly unrelated conditions such as exposure to air pollution, toxic metals, or ambient radiation. Obviously, some of those things you can control (quit smoking) and some you can't (the level of air pollution where you live). Chronic loss of sleep, poor nutrition, inadequate hydration, and continual stress all add to the burden on skin and exacerbate signs of age.

You also don't have control—yet—over your genetic profile. Most skin aging is a defect in DNA, which includes damage done by ROS and UV ray penetration but also factors in your racial background. Northern Europeans are more susceptible to visible indicators of skin aging than are, for instance, Indians or Africans. Being aware of your skin type (see the Fitzpatrick Skin Type chart on page 89) will influence how many extra measures you need to take to protect your skin from wear and tear over time.

Given all the factors that contribute to the age your skin shows, it's no wonder that people seek out products that promise age-fighting benefits. Determining the efficacy of those products means understanding the active ingredients commonly used in them, and how they work on—and in—the skin.

Scarring

Scars are a special class of skin defect because they don't affect everyone, and each one is different. Most scars diminish and fade over time, although some—specifically certain acne scarring and what are known as keloid scars—may remain prominent for life if not treated. Some scars, such as serious burn scars, may inhibit free movement of arms, legs, or your head. Dermatologists have a number of treatments at their disposal for dealing with scars, and early treatment—soon after the burn or wound seals and has healed or when acne begins to clear up—is essential for any treatment to be as effective as possible. Physicians often recommend massaging scars as soon as possible to ensure the tissue doesn't become stiff, hard, and intractable (although follow your doctor's advice because massaging a scar too early could reopen a wound), and using a topical CBD cream can help with both diminishing the long-term effect of the scar and any related inflammation and pain. Regardless of the source of the scarring, it's wise to limit your sun exposure on any scar.

The Bane of Brown Spots

Known as "solar lentigines," brown spots are inevitable as we age. We even call them age spots. Although they can be white ("guttate hypomelanosis"—the result of UV rays actually destroying the melanocytes in one small area of skin), they are more commonly brown. The brown is a result of "hyperpigmentation" as cells produce abundant melanin in response to a saturation of sunlight.

For older women, especially those who have gone through menopause, brown spots can be a source of embarrassment. Generally, doctors have responded to patient complaints about brown spots with lightening treatments such as kojic acid coupled with hydroquinone. I believe that CBD topical formulas may have an impact on these spots, and a recent experience a friend of mine had backs up that hypothesis.

She is an advocate for medical marijuana and the use of cannabinoids and, as such, she regularly receives product samples. A manufacturer sent her a CBD skin spray, and she decided to try an experiment on her own brown spots. She sprayed one arm with the spray each day for a week. On the other arm, she used her regular skincare routine. After only a week, she showed me her two arms. The difference was noticeable and significant. The sprayed arm had far fewer brown spots and actually looked, what I would call, "younger." Obviously, a much larger sample size is needed (although not too many researchers are scrambling to find a solution to brown spots), but I think this points to a cosmetic potential of CBD beauty products. It's also a treatment you can try on your own skin with a modest investment and little worry about side effects.

Skincare Products, CBD, and Aging

The challenge in using an anti-aging skincare product is that most are formulated to solve an internal problem with an external solution. As I described earlier, it's difficult for compounds to penetrate all the layers of our skin. The barrier of cells that serve as the foundation for the top layer of your epidermis, the stratum corneum, will allow the penetration of water-based molecules but prevent the passage of oil-based molecules. Ceramides—the glue that holds the cells together—are lipophilic. That means they only allow the passage of oil-based molecules, blocking water-soluble molecules. That creates a dual protection against foreign substances or molecules that might harm your system if they made it into the bloodstream. Unfortunately, it also makes it quite difficult for skincare formulas to migrate any lower than the stratum corneum, the skin's top layer. This limits the impact of most ingredients in those products.

Penetrating the Skin

There are three basic ways for an anti-aging product's active ingredient to make its way down through the skin's base layers: through ducts (such as those connected to sebaceous and sweat glands), in between cells (intercell), and through the cells themselves (intracell). This is for good reason: one of the key purposes of the skin layers is to keep outside material on the outside. The trick is to integrate ingredients with small molecules and a combination of water and fat solubility. This is where you need to be a very leery customer. If an over-the-counter product can actually penetrate to the basement layer, it will explicitly say so. Most, however, will fudge the point with language like, "Penetrates *surface* layers."

The other factor affecting compounds found in anti-aging serums, lotions, or creams is stability. Many potentially beneficial agents change or break down as soon as they are exposed to oxygen, heat, light, or certain other chemicals. This makes it a challenge to deliver those active ingredients right where they need to go.

So that leaves us with what tends to work. The three most powerful anti-aging compounds? Sunblock, a strong moisturizer, and retinoic acid.

But here's a look at the most common ingredients in cosmetic products intended to fight skin aging. The science supports some of them more than others, so consumers should be cautious about the hype used to sell these products.

- Antioxidants. Premature skin aging is caused, in no small part, by free radicals—the damaging, highly charged electrons that wreak havoc in our bodies. How do you fight free radicals? One word: antioxidants. Your body uses natural antioxidants to continually keep free radicals in check. Unfortunately, as you age, free radicals increase. That's why adding antioxidants to a skincare regimen can slow the signs of skin aging. It's also why you don't have to look very hard or far to find a skincare product boasting antioxidant ingredients. In fact, it's probably harder to find one that doesn't make the claim. You'll often see the most powerful antioxidants, such as vitamin E, vitamin C, and polyphenols such as resveratrol (a micronutrient packed with antioxidants), crowding the labels of products that claim "anti-aging" at the top of their benefits list.

CBD could be on that list too. It rivals vitamin E and even resveratrol for pure antioxidant power. But the fact remains, there is a reason why we get most of our antioxidants through our diets. It's difficult to transport something like vitamin E to the cells that most need it via a topical application. Not only are vitamins and other antioxidants fairly unstable in topical formulas—subject to deterioration by everything from oxygen to time—they are also unlikely to be carried down through the dermal barrier to where most free radical damage occurs. In general, I recommend ingesting antioxidants to enjoy the full benefit. This includes CBD. If you want to get the most out of the CBD you use, ingest capsules or tinctures.

- Copper peptides. Derived from an essential trace mineral, copper peptides are—like all peptides—fragments of proteins. These amino-acid chains play an important role in several metabolic processes, including repair and maintenance of connective tissues and structures like those found in the ECM. Cosmetic manufacturers have heartily embraced copper peptides, pointing to their effectiveness as an aid to healing wounds while keeping scar tissue to a minimum. Copper peptides in the body diminish with age, so supplementation of some sort would logically seem to be a good idea. Products containing this type of peptide can legitimately boast anti-aging properties because the peptides increase collagen and elastin production.

Copper peptides are also an effective antioxidant. But applying a topical formula with what can amount to a miniscule amount of actual copper peptides is problematic. When it comes to copper peptides, you can have too much of a good thing, so cosmetic manufacturers are likely to err on the side of caution and incorporate smaller amounts in their formulas. There is also the question of how stable copper peptides remain in a cream or lotion. That said, if you want to try out a skin moisturizer or repair serum with copper peptides, CBD would be a natural complement because copper peptides are often paired with anti-inflammatories.

- DMAE (dimethylaminoethanol). This is another widely advertised innovation in skincare products. Derived from the B vitamin choline, it has long found fans in general nutrition advocates who promote it as a mental acuity supplement. DMAE is believed to spur the production of *acetylcholine*, a neurotransmitter that can stimulate muscle contraction. Cosmetic manufacturers tout its ability to tighten and smooth skin. The other major challenge is that DMAE is most stable in an alkaline formula with a pH approaching 10. Skin is, of course, closer to neutral, with a pH of between 5.5 to 6.5. Even when that problem is overcome, I've yet to read conclusive evidence that DMAE has a lasting effect on skin tone or elasticity. Even if the claims made about supplemental DMAE are anywhere close to truth, the benefits would be more likely optimized by taking oral doses rather than using a topical formula. There is no evidence, to my knowledge, that suggests CBD and DMAE have any commonality or symbiotic effect.

- Epidermal growth factor. Known by the acronym EGF, epidermal growth factors are naturally occurring proteins found in the fibroblast cells of both plants and animals. These proteins are essential for wound and skin-damage repair. Attaching to receptors, they signal repair mechanisms and cells to swing into action, producing collagen and spurring immune responses. Theoretically, EGFs will repair wrinkling and skin discoloration and improve general skin texture. Skincare product companies were understandably excited by the potential. But in topical formulations, EGFs have yet to equal their hype. The problem is that EGFs are large molecules that are not likely to pass through the dermal barrier. It's also unlikely that a topical formulation will contain a high enough concentration of EGFs to make a substantial impact. Any formula combining EGFs and CBD most likely will do no harm, but there isn't any synergetic action between the two that provides an overarching reason for their use together.

- Kinetin. Advertised as an ingredient in many skincare products, this is derived from plants. Cosmetic companies have promoted kinetin as a less irritating alternative to retinoic acid. But, for my money, its effectiveness has yet to be proven. In plants, this compound aids in essential functions such as efficient cell division, nutrient transportation, and more. There is simply scant evidence that it does the same for human skin or that kinetin in a topical formula can reach the dermis, where it would be the most effective. Kinetin is used for medicinal preparations and helps reduce some superficial signs of aging, including fine wrinkles like those that accumulate around the eyes and mouth, dilated blood vessels near the surface of the skin, and minor uneven pigmentation. I believe there is no harm in combining kinetin with CBD, but the two don't appear to boost each other.

- MMP (matrix metalloproteinases) inhibitors. As I mentioned earlier, the role of MMP enzymes is to scavenge the components that make up the ECM—the underlying substructure that holds our skin in place and gives it texture and shape. Aging throws the balance of collagen and elastin production on one side, and MMP action on the other, out of whack. MMPs become too efficient. To make up for the deficit of collagen and elastin, MMP inhibitors slow down the action of MMP enzymes. It's a sound theory. But like a lot of medical theories, it has not borne fruit in studies. I think it probably shows the most promise at drug-level doses and in an oral delivery method. But only one MMP inhibitor drug, Periostat, has made it through clinical trials. It is FDA approved and specifically indicated for periodontitis: gum disease.

  All of that is why I'm leery of any over-the-counter formula that boasts effective MMP-inhibiting benefits. Those claims are largely unproven as far as I can see, and most studies into those formulations are conducted by and for cosmetics companies themselves. I just don't feel they hold up scientifically. However, here's an interesting aside: Research has revealed that skin inflammation increases the amount of MMP enzymes (those compounds inhibitors are trying to reduce). Because CBD has proven anti-inflammatory effects, it will logically diminish the inflammation that causes the responsive production of MMP. That's one more reason why I think a CBD formula meant for daily topical application (something like a light-bodied CBD sunscreen or CBD moisturizer) would have a small impact on suppressing MMP enzymes and keeping the skin more youthful. The CBD could be used alone or combined with MMP inhibitors.

- Peptides. Yes, it might sound like some waterborne creature, but peptides are fragments of proteins comprised of amino acids. They can be combined to create proteins, making them building blocks in the essential material for skin texture and structure. There are dozens of peptides, and specific ones appear to play a role in individual skin processes. Theoretically, peptides can regenerate older skin, reviving it to a visibly more youthful state. The mechanism behind peptides suggests they could have a beneficial impact on collagen production, counteracting some of the thinning of aging skin. They also have moisture-preserving properties, making them ideal for a topical formula. There is little clinical information about how peptides actually work in this delivery formula, or how they might work in tandem with CBD, but I think they could be a promising addition to a CBD topical formula.

- Retinoic acid. Before we can dive into the issue of retinoic acid, it's wise to step back and talk about vitamin A and retinoids at large. Retinoic acid is, in fact, metabolized from vitamin A. It is just one among several retinoids used to treat skin conditions, particularly acne. (Prescription drug retinoids include Retin-A, Tazorac, and Differin.) Synthetic retinoids are used in non-prescription, over-the-counter preparations and are converted to retinoic acid once inside skin cells. Originally, retinoic acid was isolated and used solely to treat acne because it can drastically reduce the production of sebum. But it quickly became clear that the retinoid had other beneficial effects. It improved the telltale age-related signs of sun damage, including diminishing wrinkles and reducing brown spots, and even creating firmer, smoother, younger-looking skin.

The wonderful thing about these vitamin A derivatives is that they penetrate the dermal barrier to influence cellular action directly. All retinoids trigger cellular receptors, which can spur cell turnover and collagen and elastin production. They have also been found to inhibit enzymes, such as MMPs, which break down collagen. Over-the-counter products contain weaker, synthetic versions of prescription retinoic acid. That means they'll work less quickly, with a less profound impact on skin age indicators. Look for formulas containing either retinol or retinyl palmitate in a 1 percent concentration—the strongest allowed in non-prescription products.

Several products on the market combine CBD with retinol, adding anti-inflammatory power to the retinoid's age-fighting properties. I would suggest starting with the two ingredients in separate topical formulas because I believe their powers and benefits are likelier to be more effective when each is used in isolation. I haven't seen enough evidence of how the two work together in a single formula. I would theorize that the order in which you use a retinol product and a CBD product is important. Topical retinol tends to dry out skin, while CBD is most effective when readily absorbed into the epidermis. That's why I would use a retinol product first, which would actually prepare the skin for CBD. Wait ten minutes and then apply the CBD formula. It should soak right into the skin. Keep in mind when using any formula with retinol or any form of vitamin A that it can dry out your skin and will increase photosensitivity (sensitivity to sunlight and UV rays). CBD helps reverse that sensitivity. That's why it's wise to use a sunscreen with these types of products or use them as a bedtime treatment in overnight applications.

Use a CBD moisturizing formula at night and then again in the morning.

Hyaluronic Acid

If you've seen all the hype around hyaluronic acid, a component of connective tissue, you'll know it has been heavily promoted as an ingredient in premium skincare creams. You could be forgiven for thinking that this is the latest breakthrough to come out of a lab. But in reality, hyaluronic acid is actually naturally present in our skin, a moisturizer that gloms on to moisture and helps skin stay plump and youthful. Like so many other things, the amount of hyaluronic acid decreases as we age, so supplemental amounts in topical formulas makes sense. The key is to get enough in any topical formula so that it penetrates and saturates the skin's surface. It's not going to go any deeper in most cases because the actual molecule is rather large to pass down to lower layers. It also needs to be applied daily to be continually effective. Several companies "micronize" the molecule for just that reason. You may have to dig to find out if the product does in fact contain micronized hyaluronic acid or if it is formulated with a carrier especially good for moving the ingredient deeper into the skin.

You can skip the carrier issue if you are willing to go the injectable route. Dermatologists commonly inject

hyaluronic acid into "trouble spots" to fill out skin anywhere on the body. The wonderful thing about a compound such as this is that since the body already produces
it, side effects are rare and you can introduce hyaluronic
acid to any area of skin on your body, including sensitive,
thinner spots. It is also an antibacterial, so your dermatologist can use it on burns and healing wounds with less
concern about infections.

Another benefit of this ingredient is that it partners
well with other additives to the formula, such as vitamins
and even retinol. Skincare products combining hyaluronic acid and concentrated CBD oil are promising and
are just starting to hit the market.

Sifting Through the Hype

Obviously, there is not one definitive ingredient that is
going to turn back the clock for your skin. Despite some
marketing claims, don't expect to shed years off your
appearance thanks to any individual product. A lot of the
"science" behind anti-aging beauty products is not science at all. This is because much of the research—especially among the biggest names in beauty—happens in-
house and doesn't necessarily follow rigorous scientific
methodology or peer review. Off-brand claims can be
even worse—untested, unverified, or downright wrong.

That's why it's important to cast a critical eye on label terms and product claims. Take "cosmeceutical," for example. This is a term that's been around since the 1980s and is widely used throughout the beauty industry. Understandably, consumers often assume it describes a product combining the benefits of purely cosmetic ingredients with the power of pharmaceuticals. But, in fact, it means no such thing. Any pharmaceutical is subject to strict regulatory oversight by the FDA. In reality, no government agency regulates what is or isn't a cosmeceutical, and neither the government nor industry has actually defined the word. The irony is, if any cosmeceutical actually had a measurable impact on skin cell aging, influencing the underlying mechanism of aging, it would be a powerful drug subject to a range of FDA regulations.

Government regulations are why cosmetic companies are so careful with the wording of marketing claims. In most cases, you won't find direct statements of benefit. For instance, you're unlikely to see a phrase where the manufacturer claims the product will actually reverse skin aging. Instead, it will say something more vague, such as it has an impact on skin aging. That's not to say that products labeled "anti-aging" are all bogus; they aren't. But I believe the effects may be more incremental than consumers would hope.

There is, as far as I can see, no magic fountain of youth product on the market.

Skin treatments also have their downsides. When a colleague of mine underwent her first laser skin peel, her face was quite swollen, red, and uncomfortable. Negatives from treatments such as skin resurfacing by laser or chemical peels and even microdermabrasion include severe inflammation, infections, permanent scarring, and hypo- or hyperpigmented changes. My friend had potential risks for all. She self-treated with topical hemp CBD serum twice a day on the patches where she had the most discomfort. It did a great deal to reduce her redness, swelling, and itchiness. She continued using the serum on her entire face until she healed. Now it's a part of her daily skincare routine.

I suggest a more commonsense and careful approach to maintaining healthy and youthful skin. Start with general health factors. Make sure you eat right, exercise, and get enough sleep. The biggest step you can take for slowing the signs of skin aging is to regularly use sunblock. But whenever you use sunblock, follow the instructions carefully to ensure you're applying the appropriate amount on your skin, reapplying it before it stops protecting you, and limiting other factors that could reduce the product's effectiveness (see more about selecting and using a sunblock on pages 206–210).

If you're looking to reverse established age-related skin signs, such as deep wrinkles or brown spots, I'd suggest starting with a board-certified dermatologist. There are several safe and effective treatments doctors offer to deal with one or more of the signs of aging, such as a chemical peel. Your doctor may also recommend prescription retinol. Beyond that, try out anti-aging formulas one at a time. Don't layer or combine products unless you're already sure how your skin will react to any individual product. Try out different formulations with different ingredients (including CBD) to see if one or another has a more beneficial effect on your skin's particular signs of aging.

Managing Menopause

Aging itself is enough of a challenge to your skin's condition, but women must also contend with a serious age-related life stage that can have a radical impact on skin beauty and health. Menopause initiates a quick and significant decrease in crucial hormones—specifically, estrogen and progesterone. The lower levels affect the skin in a number of ways. In the absence of normal estrogen and progesterone levels, sebaceous glands make less oil. That means drier skin. The slower growth of new blood vessels in the dermis due to lower hormone levels contributes to a dull skin tone. Menopausal women may experience slow cut and wound healing, noticeably less supple skin, thinner skin, and a general loss of youthful appearance. Added to the other mental and physical symptoms of menopause, this loss can be devastating. CBD—especially in concert with other cannabinoids—can help mitigate almost all those symptoms.

Some research indicates that oral CBD, taken with or without low-dose THC, can have a positive impact on the mood fluctuations and depression that often coincide with menopause. The combination is also effective as a sleep-aid, countering the insomnia that many menopausal women suffer through.[64]

I believe that CBD capsules or tinctures (starting with 20 milligrams divided in two daily doses) coupled with a skin moisturizer containing CBD can have a beneficial effect and will moderate many of the skin-related conditions that result from menopause.

64. Ethan Russo, Geoffrey Guy, and Philip Robson, "Cannabis, Pain, and Sleep: Lessons From Therapeutic Clinical Trials of Sativex®, a Cannabis-Based Medicine," *Chemistry & Biodiversity* 4, no. 8 (August 2007): 1729–43, https://doi.org/10.1002/cbdv.200790150.

11 · IMPROVING GENERAL HEALTH AND YOUR SKIN WITH CBD

THERE IS A VERY real truth behind the phrase "the glow of good health." How beautiful your skin appears is directly related to your overall well-being. In fact, perceptive doctors can often detect an underlying illness by observing the state of your skin and related areas like your fingernails. Basic lifestyle factors have a dramatic impact on your health and how healthy your skin looks. And CBD can, of course, have a significant impact on those factors. Topical CBD had this impact on my health, and I heard many times about my improved appearance from my nurses and colleagues.

Daily doses of ingested CBD can have a beneficial impact on overall health but also affect conditions such as inflammation that can lead to both more severe illnesses and skin

outbreaks. More precisely adjusted dosages of CBD—
sometimes in concert with THC or other cannabinoids—
can be used as part of the treatment for specific illnesses
whose symptoms include skin issues. Let's start with the
general and work our way to those particular conditions.

Inflammation

Many diseases start with, or are exacerbated by, general
or chronic inflammation. These are as diverse as arthritis,
diabetes, and depression. Inflammation plays a significant role in skin conditions ranging from acne to eczema.
It can also disrupt well-being. It's not just the actual tissue changes themselves; inflammation starts a cascading
response that can produce detrimental free radicals and
other harmful effects. The anti-inflammatory properties
of CBD have been well established through research and
in studies.[65] This makes it a valuable part of the toolbox
in fighting inflammatory autoimmune diseases—such as
lupus and psoriasis—that often result in severe skin conditions. It also makes CBD a good bet to fight any inflammatory condition in the skin or elsewhere in the body.

---

65. Sumner Burstein, "Cannabidiol (CBD) and Its Analogs: A Review
of Their Effects on Inflammation," *Bioorganic & Medicinal Chemistry* 23, no. 7 (April 2015): 1377–85, https://doi.org/10.1016/j
.bmc.2015.01.059.

Obesity

Unless you've been avoiding news reports for the last twenty years, you know that obesity is an epidemic in America. Obesity is considered a body mass index (BMI) above 30. Your doctor can provide your current BMI. Obesity leads to a host of health problems, including skin conditions. An underlying issue of obesity is, in fact, the inflammation mentioned above. Researchers studying obesity found that overweight women have an increased risk of psoriasis.[66] There also appears to be a modest connection between high caloric intake and skin cancer. Studies have found that mice kept on a restricted-calorie diet are less prone to develop skin cancers, so inferring the inverse would be logical.[67]

Excess fat deposits also increase chronic inflammation throughout the body, including in the skin and other organs. Obesity-related metabolic syndrome is a condition that results from a sedentary lifestyle and an excess of body fat. The potential effects are numerous, serious, and

---

66. Samuel Bremmer, et al., "Obesity and Psoriasis: From the Medical Board of the National Psoriasis Foundation," *Journal of the American Academy of Dermatology* 63, no. 6 (December 2010): 1058–69, https://doi.org/10.1016/j.jaad.2009.09.053.

67. Diane F. Birt, et al., "Influence of Diet and Calorie Restriction on the Initiation and Promotion of Skin Carcinogenesis in the Sencar Mouse Model," *Cancer Research* 51, no. 7 (April 1991): 1851–54, https://cancerres.aacrjournals.org/content/canres/51/7/1851.full.pdf.

include cardiovascular disease, diabetes, high blood pressure, fatty liver and gallstones, polycystic ovary disease, and sleep apnea. These are cascading conditions that can each amplify the onset and damage of the others. Oddly, despite the reputation of cannabis users, studies have shown they have a third less incidence of obesity than the general population.[68] Research published in the May 2016 issue of *Molecular and Cellular Biochemistry* has also shown that CBD plays a role in converting unhealthy white fat to healthier brown fat—which is thermogenic and responsible for burning off calories.[69] And of course, CBD is well chronicled as an inflammation fighter.

Although clinical studies are needed, there is some evidence that CBD offers the potential to diminish appetite and boost metabolism. I think weight issues are one more reason to take CBD daily in capsule or tincture form. I recommend starting out with 20 mgs taken in two daily doses, increasing by 5 to 10 mgs every five to seven days until you hit the sweet spot of tolerance without

68. Omayma Alshaarawy and James C. Anthony, "Are Cannabis Users Less Likely to Gain Weight? Results From a National 3-Year Prospective Study," *International Journal of Epidemiology* 48, no. 5 (October 2019): 1695–1700, https://doi.org/10.1093/ije/dyz044.

69. Hilal Ahmad Parray and Jong Won Yun, "Cannabidiol Promotes Browning In 3T3-L1 Adipocytes," *Molecular and Cellular Biochemistry* 416, 1–2 (May 2016): 131–39, https://doi.org/10.1007/s11010-016-2702-5.

gastrointestinal or other symptoms. I would not exceed a total of 200 milligrams in divided doses per day. Keep a detailed journal recording mood, any new symptoms, blood pressure, weight, and other metrics identified by your medical professional as relevant.

Stress

This is an area of potential application for high-dose CBD, one that has been well researched and is currently subject to many ongoing studies. Researchers are looking at CBD's potential for treatment of post-traumatic stress disorder, social anxiety disorder, and other stress-based conditions.[70] Of course, we also know from vast anecdotal evidence that a combination of CBD and THC (in the correct dosage) can alleviate general stress related to hallmark events such as financial problems or significant life changes. Stress exacerbates a vast number of diseases, including those of the skin. Acne, psoriasis, and rosacea can all be made worse when the patient is under significant stress. It's no mystery how CBD works to moderate the effects of stress. The worst byproduct of stress in our lives is a flood of hormones related to the "fight-or-flight"

---

70. Mallory J. E. Loflin, Kimberly A. Babson, and Marcel O. Bonn-Miller, "Cannabinoids as Therapeutic for PTSD," *Current Opinion in Psychology* 14 (April 2017): 78–83, https://doi.org/10.1016/j.copsyc.2016.12.001.

response hardwired into our brains. These hormones can increase inflammation, paranoia, and have other consequences like holding on to fat stores. Because the ECS plays such an important role in the regulation of hormones, the correct dose of CBD can initiate a re-balancing of the system throughout the body.

Sleep

At one time or another, you've probably heard somebody say, "I've got to get my beauty sleep." As pithy as it sounds, it's a real concern. We all need our beauty sleep when it comes to skin health. One of the chief reasons for deep sleep is for your body to restore its systems to balance and repair damage. For instance, new collagen production increases during sleep, plumping skin and filling out wrinkles. During sleep, blood flow increases out from the torso to the extremities, oxygenating arms, legs, and the face. When you don't get enough sleep, the interruption in this process leads to a dull complexion. Poor sleep or sleep deprivation significantly impacts our homeostasis, our internal hormonal balance. Dysregulations of our cortisol, thyroid, hunger, and appetite lead to risks of obesity, diabetes, high blood pressure, and poor immune response to infections.

If you regularly get less than seven hours of restorative sleep a night, it's probably taking a toll on your skin. The

Centers for Disease Control and Prevention reports that a third of adults get too little sleep each day.[71] The market for sleep remedies, prescription and otherwise, is billions of dollars strong and growing. Many experts consider this an epidemic because it's a relatively recent cultural phenomenon. On average, we sleep two hours less a night than our relatives did a century ago. That lack of regenerating downtime means more inflammation in the body and possibly more frequent and severe allergic responses, such as contact dermatitis. Just as good sleep spurs collagen production, sleep deprivation breaks down collagen and elastin more quickly than normal.

Preliminary research indicates that CBD and cannabinoids can serve as a safe, natural sleep aid. Not only do they help with pain and anxiety—two key reasons that people lose sleep—but some researchers believe they interact positively with parts of the brain responsible for sleep.[72] Interestingly, CBD receptors are sparsely located in the brainstem, the lowest part of our brain which controls

---

71. Yong Liu, et al., "Prevalence of Healthy Sleep Duration among Adults—United States, 2014," *Morbidity and Mortality Weekly Report*, Centers for Disease Control and Prevention 65, no. 6 (February 2016): 137–41, http://dx.doi.org/10.15585/mmwr .mm6506a1.

72. Scott Shannon, et al., "Cannabidiol in Anxiety and Sleep: A Large Case Series," *The Permanente Journal* 23 (2019): n.p., https://doi .org/10.7812/TPP/18-041.

our breathing, swallowing, and heart rate. This is in contrast to the "mu" opioid receptors, which are prevalent in the brainstem and serve as primary binding sites for most narcotics and sedatives. The co-location and stimulation of these opioid receptors in our brainstem places our lives at risk with respiratory depression or respiratory failure even with occasional use. CBD and THC are safer and differentiated from opioid drugs. If you are developing lung disease such as COPD or have sleep apnea, discuss CBD with your physician specialist as a potential sleep aid.

CBN as CBD Alternative

Although CBD has received the lion's share of press in recent years, cannabinol (CBN) is being investigated as a possibly useful—and in some cases, more powerful—complement or alternative to CBD. CBN is a converted form of THC, essentially THC that has been oxidized. It may be mildly psychoactive, but this is a point of debate among experts. Unlike CBD, CBN binds directly to CB2 receptors and is thought to play a role in interacting with CB1 receptors.

A 2008 study published in the *Journal of Natural Products* revealed that CBN, along with four other cannabinoids (CBD, THC, CBG, and CBC) showed strong antibacterial activity against methicillin-resistant *Staphy-*

lococcus aureus (MRSA).[73] A separate 2016 study published in the journal *Neural Regeneration Research*[74] and an earlier 2004 University of Washington study both showed CBN's potential for delaying symptom onset in mice with amyotrophic lateral sclerosis (ALS),[75] illustrating the dramatic potential that seems to exist for this particular cannabinoid.

Although I've focused on CBD in this book, it's important that anyone looking to maximize his or her skin or general health keep a close eye on emerging research—specifically in the benefits of related cannabinoids and discoveries regarding the entourage effect. I believe in the near future we are going to learn much more about how specific cannabinoids can work in concert for targeted health results.

73. Giovanni Appendino, et al., "Antibacterial Cannabinoids from *Cannabis sativa*: A Structure-Activity Study," *Journal of Natural Products* 71, no. 8 (August 2008): 1427–30, https://doi.org/10 .1021/np8002673.

74. Sabrina Giacoppo and Emanuela Mazzon, "Can Cannabinoids be a Potential Therapeutic Tool in Amyotrophic Lateral Sclerosis?" *Neural Regeneration Research* 11, no. 12 (December 2016): 1896–99, https://doi.org/10.4103/1673-5374.197125.

75. Patrick Weydt, et al., "Cannabinol Delays Symptom Onset in SOD1 (G93A) Transgenic Mice Without Affecting Survival," *Amyotrophic Lateral Sclerosis and Frontotemporal Degeneration* 6, no. 3 (September 2005): 182–84, https://doi .org/10.1080/14660820510030149.

Nutrition

We know how important antioxidants are for skin health; they are essential to nullifying the damage done by free radicals. Left on their own, free radicals can lead to skin damage ranging from irregular pigmentation to skin cancer. The best antioxidants come from diet, foods like blueberries, and cold-water fish. But you need much more than just antioxidants. A healthy, balanced diet includes abundant fresh and cooked vegetables and fruit, which deliver a range of vitamins and minerals that play a role in skin health. Equally important are sources of protein. Proteins are the building blocks of skin and essential for the constant cellular turnover that occurs in your skin. Lean, natural sources of protein are best, including meat and chicken that is free of antibiotics or other chemicals. You can also get protein from dairy products, beans, seeds, and nuts. Biotin, a B complex vitamin, is especially important for skin development and health. This is found in egg yolks, lentils, cauliflower, and bananas, among other foods. The vitamin strengthens the skin structure (as well as hair and nails).

However, CBD can be just as good of a source of natural antioxidants in both topical and ingested forms. And your diet can be another way to introduce different cannabinoids and a wider spectrum of beneficial compounds into your body—specifically by juicing parts of the cannabis plant or eating hempseeds. This is an area of exploration that may seem a little far out there, but I think it offers a lot of upside to people willing to take the time and effort to seek out the raw ingredients and prepare them.

Hempseeds are a highly nutritious addition to any diet, though they may be hard to find where you live. They contain a range of vitamins, including A, D, E and several B vitamins. They are also good sources of minerals such as zinc and magnesium and high in fiber. Eat them as a snack or mix them into meals, from oatmeal to chili.

Cannabis leaves are the perfect complement to hempseeds and ideal for juicing. Obviously, this is not an option if you don't live in a state that allows at least medical marijuana. However, if you can obtain cannabis leaves for juicing, you'll enjoy a bountiful source of antioxidants, omega fats, full-spectrum cannabinoids, and even protein. And you won't have to worry about getting high; the "buds" of the plant are not juiced, and the leaves contain a form of THC (THCA) that is not psychoactive.

I've mentioned this but it's worth repeating: Any discussion of nutrition in relation to skin health has to include those foods that are not good for the skin. Start with processed sugars. Candy bars and other sweets are fine as an occasional treat, but as a regular part of your diet, they can help raise insulin sensitivity. The resulting high levels of glucose circulating in the bloodstream can do enormous damage to cells throughout the body, including in the skin. High-sodium, packaged snacks, such as potato chips, are also bad for general health and the skin. Fried foods can increase the number of free radicals in your system and add to skin cell damage.

Smoking

We all know smoking is harmful, but smokers find it almost impossible to break the habit. If you're a smoker, I don't think I need to tell you—and I'm not here to pass judgement—that there are few worse things you can do to yourself in terms of both general well-being and skin health. In addition to the many serious health problems smoking can cause, it prematurely ages skin by interrupting the cellular process of skin cell turnover. Studies show that smoking also significantly increases your risk of skin cancer.[76] The answer is to stop, but that's easier said than done. However, a 2018 study found that CBD was effective in preventing relapses among alcohol- or cocaine-addicted rats.[77] There is a modest amount of evidence that CBD oil has the potential to help smokers quit.

---

76. Sofie A. E. De Hertog, et al., "Relation Between Smoking and Skin Cancer," *Journal of Clinical Oncology* 19, no. 1 (January 2001): 231–38, https://doi.org/10.1200/JCO.2001.19.1.231.

77. Gustavo Gonzalez-Cuevas, et al., "Unique Treatment Potential of Cannabidiol," 2036–45, https://doi.org/10.1038/s41386-018-0050-8.

This is a good place to clear up some confusion about smoking versus vaping. Many recreational marijuana users smoke cannabis to get high. There is evidence that the cannabinoids inhaled when smoking pot offer some protection against carcinogens that could affect the lungs (although I'm definitely not in favor of smoking anything, including marijuana). If you are set on inhaling your cannabinoids, vaping is thought to be a better alternative to smoking since it typically does not contain all the contaminants found in smoke and you can control the dose. Therapeutic vaping cartridges—those meant specifically for inhaling cannabinoids—are normally formulated to limit other ingredients beyond the carrier medium. Vaping can be especially good for treating bothersome itching and for relieving pain. However, vaping can also be fraught with danger and has come under significant scrutiny due to associated deaths and serious side effects because of additives. It is imperative that you ensure the quality of the product and consult with a specialist before embarking on a treatment plan that incorporates vaping.

Treat the Condition, Treat the Skin

There are several health issues and diseases that can have a big impact on your skin. Fortunately, the skin symptoms related to these conditions can be diminished with the help of CBD. This is not to say that CBD is the cure for the diseases listed below, but it can be an effective resource in the treatment plan for any of them.

Allergies

There are two ways allergies affect the state of your skin. Itching is a common symptom, and it can lead to scratching that inflames or even causes infections in the skin. Your skin is also subject to *allergic contact dermatitis*, a condition triggered by direct interaction with an allergen. Because CBD is an immune-system modulator working through the pervasive ECS, and because allergies are essentially overreactions of the immune system to a perceived threat, it makes sense that CBD could curb that exaggerated response and ease symptoms. The cannabinoid has been shown to curb the action of mast cells and the production of histamines that cause so many of the symptoms of an allergy attack. These same properties make CBD a possible adjunct to therapies for treating asthma, although its efficacy for that disease has not yet been proven in research.

In the interest of full disclosure, there is a small incidence of allergic reactions to cannabis itself. This can be caused by contaminants such as fungus or mold in the plant material, although it most often happens with physical exposure to the plant, its pollen, or smoking marijuana. Some allergic reactions have been chronicled in response to eating hempseeds. There is far less chance of an allergic reaction if you're taking an isolated cannabinoid such as CBD. However, in all cases, I prefer that patients, and anyone using cannabinoids or medical marijuana in any form, introduce it slowly and carefully. Monitor for any adverse reactions, and let your physician know immediately if they occur.

Anxiety Disorders

It may seem counterintuitive, but any anxiety disorder, from ADHD to PTSD and beyond, can lead to flare-ups of existing skin conditions such as rosacea, psoriasis, acne, and others. Studies exploring CBD oil's impact on general and specific anxiety point to the cannabinoid's potential to lessen the severity and frequency of symptoms—including related skin outbreaks.[78] If you have been diagnosed with any anxiety disorder, it's well worth checking with your general physician and therapist to investigate how CBD might be used in your personal treatment plan.

78. Lauren R. M. Eagleston, et al., "Cannabinoids in Dermatology: A Scoping Review," *Dermatology Online Journal* 24, no. 6 (June 2018): 1–17, https://www.semanticscholar.org/paper/Cannabinoids-in-dermatology%3A-a-scoping-review.-Eagleston-Kalani/0f25c04e84ec93462a83e6541fd3a878643e8aa1; Tóth, et al., "Cannabinoid Signaling in the Skin: Therapeutic Potential of the 'C(ut)annabinoid' System." *Molecules* 24, no. 5 (March 2019): 918. https://doi.org/10.3390/molecules24050918.

It's important not to self-medicate with CBD, especially in concert with THC. The wrong dosage or usage of these compounds can worsen anxiety.

Arthritis

Not all forms of arthritis cause skin problems, but the ones that do can wreak havoc. For instance, rheumatoid arthritis can cause a characteristic skin rash and less common *vasculitis*, which are pronounced veins near the surface of the skin similar to varicose veins. *Psoriatic arthritis* is even more devastating for the skin, causing a widespread itchy, scaly, and sometimes painful skin rash, as well as weakened nail structure. CBD can help with both conditions. The cannabinoid's pain-relieving properties are well chronicled and can lessen the pain from a rash and the underlying arthritic condition. What's more, CBD fights back against inflammatory responses, which are immune system reactions that mark any kind of arthritis.

This is a case where transdermal CBD patches coupled with a twice-daily dose of 10 mg CBD capsules can have a noticeable effect on the pain and severity of a disease. This is true for joint diseases of all kinds. Transdermal patches are coated with a medium that will carry CBD down through the skin to underlying muscle and tissue. These patches are also available in varying dosages and in combinations such as CBD-THC, CBN, THCA, and others. I think they offer a lot of promise for not only arthritis sufferers but also for anyone suffering from conditions that affect the joints, such as fibromyalgia, lupus, and bursitis.

Autoimmune Disorders

If you suffer from a disease such as lupus or fibromyalgia, or know someone who does, you know the life-altering pain, suffering, and fatigue that go along with chronic autoimmune diseases. You will also be aware of the skin pain and rashes that can accompany this family of disorders. For instance, a common symptom of fibromyalgia is a red, raised, bumpy rash (most likely due to prescription medication side effects) that is sensitive to the touch and can be painful. Lupus is also associated with rashes and exceptional skin sensitivity, including extreme sensitivity to the sun's UV rays. These skin symptoms go hand-in-glove with fatiguing joint inflammation and pain.

Transdermal CBD patches can help with joint pain and discomfort. A CBD topical lotion may calm rashes and other autoimmune condition skin symptoms, but don't be alarmed if the topical preparation does not resolve the issue; the underlying condition may cause the symptom regardless of superficial treatment. A topical cream combining THC and CBD may, however, lessen pain associated with the skin condition. Sublingual CBD tinctures and oral capsules in conjunction with topicals may be impactful to decrease the length or severity of symptoms through the workings of our ECS. I highly recommend a thoughtful discussion with your specialist about incorporating CBD in your treatment plan.

Diabetes

This serious disease inhibits the body's ability to metabolize glucose and, in doing that, creates problems with sufferers' skin. At various stages of pre-diabetes and diabetes (Type I and Type II), a person's skin may show discolored patches (*xanthoma*); areas of overly dry skin; itchy, dry skin on the legs; hard, thick, and waxy skin on the hands; colored spots on the shins; clusters of small, red bumps or larger patches of angry red or purple bumps; and an inability to properly heal cuts and wounds on the extremities. But we already know CBD's effectiveness against inflammation, something that is an exacerbating factor in developing the insulin resistance that leads to diabetes. A CBD moisturizer used in conjunction with twice-daily doses of CBD, starting at 20 milligrams a day, may provide relief for some symptoms of diabetes and moderate the disease's severity, not to mention directly treating associated skin conditions.

Other Skin Conditions

Many skin problems are the result of other conditions and disease. In some cases, because the underlying issue is the cause, it may not be possible to completely resolve the skin issue. However, even in those cases, topical (and sometimes oral) CBD can provide at least some measure of relief and healing. In the best-case scenario, CBD cream may lessen the severity of scarring.

Surgical Scars

Healing or reducing the severity of surgical and major wound scarring is an area of obvious interest for surgeons and physicians knowledgeable in the use of CBD and other cannabinoids. Clinical studies are lacking, but anecdotal information suggests that a CBD ointment used on fresh scarring or even an open wound may assist healing. This would seem to be commonsense given CBD's well-chronicled anti-inflammatory and antibacterial properties. Of course, the other side to scarring, whether from surgery or a wound, is the pain associated with healing. A 2017 study described in the *Journal of Pain Symptom Management* showed that CBD topical application significantly decreased the need for opioid pain management in serious wounds.[79]

Radiation

Radiation therapy can coarsen, thicken, and inflame skin at the focal point of treatment. Topical CBD can't reverse all those changes, but it can provide relief and anti-inflammatory benefits. Adding CBD oil to healing ointment can be a simple way to boost whatever product you're using. However, consult closely with your radiation oncologist, because in some cases, it may be advisable to wait at least several hours after a treatment before applying the ointment.

Chemotherapy

Some side effects of chemotherapy affect the skin. Dry, itchy, red patches are common with this cancer treatment as well as rash and sun sensitivity. The severity of all these can be lessened with topical applications of CBD cream or ointment. Of course, oral or sublingual CBD can also help with other symptoms, most pointedly the nausea that is

---

79. Vincent Maida and Jason Corban, "Topical Medical Cannabis: A New Treatment for Wound Pain—Three Cases of Pyoderma Gangrenosum," *Journal of Pain and Symptom Management* 54, no. 5 (November 2017): 732–36, https://doi.org/10.1016/j .jpainsymman.2017.06.005.

so common—and can be so devastating—with chemotherapy. Many sufferers find noticeable relief by ingesting
a combination of CBD and THC in doses starting around
10 milligrams of each, increasing as necessary if tolerated.
This has the added benefit of spurring appetite, something that is often diminished with chemotherapy drugs.

Keloid Scars

These are caused by overactive scar tissue and can result
from any insult to the skin. Keloid scars appear as raised,
overlarge areas of tissue growth. Although CBD formulas may provide some modest relief, treating keloid scars
requires a medical or surgical technique that involves
particular expertise and equipment.

Burns

Treating burns is a case where the type of CBD you use is
vitally important. Choose a pure, full-spectrum CBD. To
be most effective in treating first- or second-degree burns,
the cannabinoid should be combined with terpenes, most
specifically linalool, which will provide a cooling sensation
to the injured area. Treating the burn quickly is key to preventing lasting skin damage. The CBD acts on many fronts
in fighting a burn on the skin, providing some element
of pain relief, an antibiotic action to head off infection,
and anti-inflammatory benefits to stop further damage

and pain. I highly recommend concurrent medical attention for burns because the severity of injury is often deeper than the eye can see.

Obviously, getting the dose right is critical to using CBD as part of the treatment for any illness. But it's also essential that you buy CBD products from reputable sources. Whether you're using capsules, oils, tinctures, or topical preparations, you need to trust the contents of the product. Pure or full-spectrum CBD from hemp plants is, I believe, the best type of CBD that should be used to treat medical conditions. Unfortunately, the booming popularity of this compound has come with a lot of fly-by-night manufacturers who market products of dubious quality and consistency. Now more than ever, it's essential to be a smart consumer. The next chapter is focused on helping you get the highest CBD products at the best value.

12 · SHOPPING SMART FOR CBD SKINCARE PRODUCTS

SKINCARE PRODUCTS CONTAINING CBD are like any other beauty products: they are most often seductively packaged in alluring containers and marketed with scintillating promises of regenerated, reinvigorated, healthier skin. The hype is often even more hyperbolic than usual because this is CBD's moment. It has grown in popularity to become a much-touted ingredient in products from sunscreen to sparkling water. Some CBD manufacturers and treatment providers are calling it the next great cure-all. Those factors make it incredibly tough for the average consumer to sift through slick packaging and even slicker promotional copy. Being an informed shopper is vitally important.

The experience of walking into a cosmetics store or the beauty department of a larger retailer is an exercise in sensory overload. Sophisticated product and display case designs vie for your attention, while the elegant perfumes of the vast number of products lead you by the nose. It's all in service of displacing common sense, of denying the fact that much of what is being sold can be had for a tenth of the price in the more downscale, less attractive aisle of your local drugstore.

Complicating the picture is that you have to decode the usual beauty-product ingredient lists. You have to figure out if the ingredients work for you and determine the quantity and purity of any CBD in the formula. And all this doesn't even cover shopping for CBD in capsules, tinctures, or a topical formula, much less the DIY option of creating your own custom formula.

Making the right choices isn't just a matter of getting the maximum health benefit from any product you buy; it's also a case of economic reality. The truth is, CBD in ingestible form, and the topical skincare products that include it as a key ingredient, are often prohibitively expensive. Fortunately, a few simple guidelines and rules will aid you in the search for the highest-quality and best value-for-money beauty products and supplemental CBD.

Honesty in the Marketplace

Being an informed consumer means determining the purity and concentration of any CBD product you buy.

It also means wading through an even greater number of general skincare product terms and claims. For instance, have you ever read or heard that common phrase, "Seven out of ten doctors recommend …"? It's long been a claim for promoting products, but few consumers ask themselves, "What doctors and how did they come to their conclusions?"

To start with, cosmetic manufacturers often keep both researchers and clinical medical professionals on the payroll. The more accurate claim in many cases might be, "Seven out of ten doctors we paid recommended our product as safe and effective." Not exactly a ringing endorsement.

The other myth in any health or beauty product—from moisturizer to CBD capsules—is that "Studies show …" Again, the question is, "What studies?" Companies inside and outside the beauty industry frequently cite studies that the company itself or the industry sponsored. Called "proprietary," these studies are often performed at a manufacturer's in-house lab by on-staff personnel. They are rarely peer reviewed and, not surprisingly, even more rarely negative in their outcomes. Those realities mean that the legitimacy of the results claimed by the studies is questionable. Internal studies sometimes lack the rigor of, for instance, FDA research. Anytime a manufacturer promotes a product benefit because "studies show" that it has been proven, always ask yourself, "Which studies, and performed by whom?"

Before you can consider, accept, or debunk a product's claim, you need to start with the actual products that are right for you.

Product Format

The first issue you'll deal with when shopping for topical skincare products (whether they contain CBD or not) is the delivery formulation. Generally, you'll choose between ointments, creams, and lotions. All are basically oil suspended in water through the magic of chemistry; the difference is the amount of fat to water.

An ointment is generally about 80 percent oil and 20 percent water, making it greasier and longer lasting on the surface of the skin. A cream is a 50-50 blend of oil and water. Creams absorb more quickly and are easier to spread on the skin. A lotion is lighter and has more water to oil than a cream.

Prescription medicine can be, and is, integrated into all three bases. In the case of medical applications, your physician will lead you to one or the other. Each has pros and cons. Creams are generally used over larger areas and on conditions that are consistently moist. They are better for hidden areas where skin tends to contact skin, such as under breasts or in armpits. In contrast, ointments tend to be used on drier skin conditions because they trap moisture and hold it. Because they sit on the skin longer, ointments are usually the carrier of choice for formulas meant to penetrate deeply.

CBD can be incorporated into these formulations. However, because the cannabinoid is not regulated by the FDA, any consumer has to verify the amount, potency, and interactions of CBD in a given skincare product.

Skincare Product Glossary

Any product label can be daunting to decode, and skincare and beauty products are no less so. The list below is not exhaustive, but it does contain the most common skincare product ingredients, which should help you understand the products you find at retail. These ingredients may have properties that cross several categories. The examples listed do not represent an endorsement for safety; I have discovered some contribute to my own skin sensitivities.

- Binders. Exactly as it sounds, a skincare product binder is meant to hold specific elements of the formula together—most pointedly, oil and water. Examples of common binders include polysorbates, palmitates, and ceteareth 20.

- Buffers. Skincare buffers serve an important role in making any formula skin friendly. Buffers balance the pH of the product to better match the nearly neutral pH of our skin. Another way to put it is that the buffer neutralizes acids in the formula, preventing them from irritating the skin. Examples include citric acid, triethanolamine, and sodium bicarbonate—better known as baking soda.

- Emollients. This word comes from the Latin *mollire*, which means "to soften."[80] But emollients are not just softeners. They also protect the skin with a barrier that keeps moisture in and some contaminants out. A great number of emollients are found in nature, and this class includes coconut oil, shea and cocoa butters, olive oil, and beeswax, as well as the chemicals cetyl alcohol and triethylhexanoin, among many others.

- Emulsifiers. Just as binders hold opposing ingredients together, emulsifiers keep dissimilar substances from separating, preventing any skincare product from separating into its constituent ingredients. The most common emulsifiers you'll find among label listings include polysorbates, laureth-4, and potassium cetyl sulfate.

---

80. "Emollient," Online Etymology Dictionary, Douglas Harper, n.d., https://www.etymonline.com/word/emollient#etymonline _v_5812.

- Humectants. These are a type of moisturizer that pulls water out of the air to keep the top layers of the skin hydrated. They include both synthetic versions like propylene glycol and silicone compounds, and natural ingredients such as aloe, hyaluronic acid, and glycerin.

- Surfactants. Surfactants are a class of compounds that generally function to hold ingredients in a formula together—although many have other purposes as well. They can be divided into those that blend with oil (lipophilic), those that blend better with water (hydrophilic), and those that repel water (hydrophobic). Detergent surfactants are cleaning agents. Foaming surfactants create a scrubbing action and are conditioning agents that moisturize and protect. *Solubilizers* help blend active ingredients into oils (an example is skin toner). In one way or another, most surfactants are cleansers and range from extremely mild to extremely harsh. Common surfactants you're likely to see on labels include sodium palmate or palmitate, dodecylbenzenesulfonate, disodium lauryl sulfosuccinate, sodium lauryl sulfate, sodium cocoyl glutamate, alpha-Olefin sulfonate, cocoamidopropyl betaine, and ammonium laureth sulfate.

- Preservatives. As in many consumer products, skin-care preservatives serve two roles—keeping the product shelf life stable and preventing growth of or killing harmful bacteria and mold in the formula. Preservatives can be synthetic or natural. The most common skincare formula preservatives are propylene glycol, benzyl alcohol, formaldehyde, phenoxyethanol, and parabens.

- Texturizers. As the name implies, these ingredients add a pleasing texture, such as smoothness and creaminess, that not only makes the product more alluring, they also help in applying the product. Texturizers include polymers such as polyethylene glycol, pentaerythrityl tetraoctanoate, caprylic and succinic triglycerides, sodium chloride, polysorbate 20 and 80, dimethicone, and cyclomethicone.

The Essentials

In addition to any prescription or over-the-counter preparations you buy for a specific condition, you should be shopping for three baseline skincare products: a mild cleanser, a simple moisturizer, and a long-lasting sunblock. With all these products, knowing key terms will help you find the best for your skin and health.

- Hypoallergenic. This indicates that the formula has been developed without known allergens. Of course, there's an argument to be made that given the trend toward more benign, organic ingredients, most skincare formulations from reputable manufacturers are unlikely to cause an allergic reaction. Hypoallergenic products are not regulated by the FDA. What is regulated is the requirement to list the ingredients so consumers may avoid products that can cause them harm. Still, the term isn't necessarily misleading and there's no real downside to seeing it on a product label.

- Non-comedogenic. This is one of the most important claims a skincare product can carry because it essentially means the product was formulated specifically to avoid blocking hair follicle pores and making outbreaks of acne worse. (Comedones—the singular is *comedo*—are what are commonly known as blackheads, the visual indicators of blocked pores.) If you suffer from intermittent or chronic acne, keep an eye out for this term when shopping for any skincare product.

- pH-balanced. Healthy skin is close to neutral pH (balanced evenly between acidic and alkaline). Consequently, ideal skincare products are close to neutral, or match the skin's ideal pH to avoid causing irritation.

- Soap-free. Most traditional soaps contain alkaline detergents (originally, ingredients like lye). Alkaline ingredients can irritate and dry out sensitive skin, so soap-free cleansers are meant to be gentler. Be aware that if your skin is sensitive, you might also have an issue with synthetic replacements.

- Unscented. This term is meant to indicate a more natural formulation that doesn't include chemicals used specifically to create an aroma. The product may include certain ingredients that mask less-desirable odors produced by other ingredients, but the goal is to create a neutral fragrance and a formulation that is less likely to irritate the skin or offend anyone's sense of smell.

Buying CBD Products Step by Step

Anytime you're consuming part of a plant, it's a great idea to look for organic options. That is even more important in shopping for CBD or other cannabinoids. Cannabis readily takes up whatever it finds in the soil, from plain nutrients to toxic heavy metals such as lead or potentially carcinogenic elements such as pesticide residue. Even chemical fertilizers can break down and add undesirable components to the plant. CBD, THC, and other cannabinoids and related compounds will be clearly marked "organic" if that is how they were grown and harvested.

The word means no chemicals were used in the cultivation, harvesting, or processing of the plant material. Just be prepared that any organic option requires more attention in the field and in cannabinoid extraction, and will therefore be more expensive than non-organic options.

The first step in finding the right CBD product— whether you're searching for the ideal beauty formula or a more general health offering—is deciding on the delivery method that will work best for you. Most topical formulas will affect only the top layer of skin and are best used to treat simple outbreaks on the surface. CBD in products like sunscreen can also help keep the epidermis healthy and will have some impact on reversing or preventing cell damage to that layer.

More penetrating formulas meant to ease joint soreness or address the connective tissue damage from diseases such as arthritis and fibromyalgia will deliver any CBD in the formula into the bloodstream. Ingestible forms of CBD are plentiful, and many conditions (as I've discussed elsewhere) are best addressed by a combination of topical applications and CBD supplements. Although in any state where cannabis is legal you'll be able to choose from a range of CBD edibles as varied as gummies, capsules, or even chocolates, those products may not be available where there is local or state pushback against CBD availability and where pot is still illegal. CBD capsules and tinctures are, however, available in almost every state.

Sunscreen and Sunblock

The prevailing consensus among dermatology professionals is that one of the best preventative measures you can take against serious skin problems is to use sunblock or sunscreen daily. Before you can pick from among the vast number of products available, you need to understand the basics about protecting your skin from the sun's UV rays.

First and foremost, it's important to know the difference between the two: sunblock contains compounds that physically block the sun—like putting armor over your skin—while sunscreen contains chemicals designed to screen the UVA and UVB rays, essentially stopping them from harming skin cells from the moment they penetrate the epidermis. Some products combine both physical blockers, such as zinc oxide, with chemical screens such as avobenzone or octinoxate.

Regardless of whether you choose a sunblock or sunscreen, it's essential that you buy a product that protects against both UVB and UVA rays (they are usually clearly labeled "broad spectrum"). Adding CBD to sun protection is a natural combination because CBD counteracts inflammation and other detrimental effects from the sun's rays. The CBD concentration in any product of this sort should be substantial—100 milligrams per ounce of sunscreen is a good baseline.

There are several other issues to consider. Different sunscreen formulations are meant for different applications. For instance, long-lasting "sport" products are meant to be effective even after water exposure or heavy sweating. They are bound to be somewhat sticky and may be uncomfortable under clothing. Lighter-bodied moisturizing sunscreens are better choices for daily use after a shower because they are far less sticky and greasy. The variation in textures, carrier mediums, and formulations is why it's ideal to keep two or more sunscreens on hand for different situations. Use at least one every day, preferably applying it as you get out of the shower and again during the day.

Play close attention to the effective duration of protection. As a general guide, apply sunscreen at least thirty minutes before going out into the sun and reapply before the time recommended on the label. (That clock starts ticking as soon as you put it on, *not* at the first exposure to direct sun.)

As I mentioned earlier, SPF is a key factor in choosing sun protection. Unfortunately, it's also woefully misunderstood among most consumers. I think most people consider it an absolute measure of how much sun protection any given formula offers. That's not the case. Actually, it is much less precise and more variable than that. An acronym for "sun protection factor," SPF is a ballpark measure of how long the formula will be effective in blocking or screening UV rays.

This is how SPF is calculated: Say you're fair skinned and would likely start burning after 10 minutes in direct sunlight. If you're using a 30 SPF sunscreen, that product will—all things being equal—protect for thirty times your burn limit, or three hundred minutes, before it needs to be reapplied. Now this is the really important part: Only the actual ingredients—not the SPF—determine how much and what UV rays are blocked or screened. Higher SPF formulations block slightly more rays (for instance, research shows that 15 SPF blocks about 93 percent of UVB rays, while the much more impressive-sounding 50 SPF blocks about 98 percent).[81]

There are, of course, other complicating factors. If you have particularly dry skin, you may absorb the formula more quickly and diminish how long it is effective (a good case for buying a formula rich with humectants). If you sweat a lot, you may eliminate the product more

81. Brummitte Dale Wilson, Summer Moon, and Frank Armstrong, "Comprehensive Review of Ultraviolet Radiation and the Current Status on Sunscreens," *The Journal of Clinical and Aesthetic Dermatology* 5, no. 9 (September 2012): 18–23, https://www.ncbi.nlm.nih.gov/pmc/articles/PMC3460660/.

quickly than normal, depending on the formula you've purchased. Regardless of the given product, one of the most common mistakes all consumers make is under-applying sun protection. Thoroughly slather on any sun protection formula, coating every crevice and fold of skin.

No matter what product you buy, be a label reader. There are some controversial ingredients in sunscreens, such as chemicals and compounds that the FDA is currently reviewing. For instance, to make sunblock more convenient and comfortable for users, manufacturers "micronize" physical blockers such as zinc and titanium oxide. There is concern that these nanoparticles can infiltrate the pores and skin follicles in the skin to enter the bloodstream, possibly leading to detrimental health effects. Unfortunately, the vast majority of sunblock products contain nanoparticles. You won't be able to determine that because that fact doesn't have to be included on the label or anywhere on the product. It is, however, worth contacting companies directly or opting for those that explicitly say their products do not contain nanoparticles. (Be aware that in the absence of nanoparticles, you'll need to reapply the product more often.)

That leaves sunscreen, which raises other concerns. The most pressing ingredient of concern is oxybenzone, a chemical that absorbs readily through the skin and can have adverse effects on sex hormones, potentially causing a range of health concerns. That's why I would suggest avoiding products that contain oxybenzone.

Fortunately, these days sun protection is not limited to sunscreen and sunblock. You can buy moisturizers and even makeup with SPF ratings. Regardless of the product you buy, opting for one with CBD is a great option. Honestly, there can be a bit of sticker shock with any high-quality sunscreen, especially if it contains CBD, other cannabinoids, or related compounds such as terpenes. However, it is money well spent. Sun protection is the first—and essential—line of defense for your skin.

Facial Cleansers

As consumers, it's easy to get enchanted by a class of products that seem to make sense in our lives. Unfortunately, some of these products can be complicated options where a very basic alternative would serve just as well. Body and facial cleansers fall into this category. Certainly, for people suffering with specific skin conditions, a specialized cleanser may be necessary and valuable. But for most people with average skin (not too oily or too dry), a gentle bar soap for the body and warm water and a washcloth for the face may suffice. But I do realize that people often enjoy the clean feeling facial cleansers provide. And many products make claims of doing more than cleaning, such as increasing circulation to the uppermost layer of skin.

The trick, especially on your face, is to use a cleanser appropriate for your particular skin traits. Harsher is rarely better in the case of cleansers. I think we sometimes make the mistake of feeling like a bracing cleanser that leaves our skin tingling is the sign of a product that is really working. In many instances, that's actually a sign of a product that is working far too hard. Cleansers are a skincare class where synthetics have really afforded an advantage over traditional "natural" ingredients. True soap is made from highly alkaline—caustic—lye combined with fatty acids. It can be very abusive to skin, especially thinner facial skin. Today's "soaps" often contain no lye or similar alkaline but instead use manmade detergent or other surfactant alternatives.

That's why picking the right cleanser for your face comes down to picking the right ingredients. If you have oily skin, apply a lot of makeup, or get very dirty during the workday, look for strong soap or synthetic surfactants. These include sodium cocoate, sodium palm kernelate, sodium palmate, sodium lauryl sulfate, or sodium dodecylbenzene sulfonate. If your skin tends to be what you would call "normal" or slightly dry on occasion, opt for milder surfactants such as sodium laureth sulfate, ammonium lauroyl isenthionate, caprylic acid, or polysorbate 85 or 60. If hunting through the small-print list of ingredients on a label is too much, you can usually draw reasonable conclusions from the company's own descriptions. "Heavy-duty" or "strong" means harsh and best for oily skin, while "mild" or "gentle" usually means exactly that, a cleanser better suited to dry or sensitive skin.

Moisturizers

Most people understand the need for moisturizers; they are a way to protect the top layer of skin from cracking that could lead to infections and unattractively dry skin (although counterintuitive, even people with oily skin may need a moisturizer). In any case, not all moisturizers are created equal. Some are formulated specifically for extremely dry skin while others are meant for the delicate skin on the face. Several manufacturers are creating moisturizers infused with CBD; a couple have even created moisturizing sunscreens with CBD. As a bonus, several of these forego any synthetic additives, using just plant-based humectants and emollients. Fair warning though, there is a reason for synthetic beauty product ingredients. Chemical humectants and emollients serve their purposes extremely well because they are refined just for those purposes. Natural alternatives may need to be applied more often and may not have the same feel of the products you're used to.

The moisturizer that is right for you comes down to your skin type and what you want the moisturizer to do.

If you have dry skin, you can opt for an oil-based product, perhaps one with other rich, waxy ingredients such as shea butter. Truly oily skin may not require a moisturizer. However, if you use an astringent cleanser because of your skin, you may be stripping oils from it and drying your skin out. In that case, a lightweight water-based moisturizer that is not as rich might do your skin justice. As with all new beauty products, whether you're switching to a product containing CBD or just trying out a new moisturizer, I strongly recommend you test out the product on a discreet patch of skin, such as the back of your neck, to determine if you'll have any reaction to that particular formulation.

Quality Considerations

Whatever product you're considering and whatever form it takes, you should research any CBD product to verify its potency and purity. I recommend the following steps toward that goal:

1. Request the COA
   A Certificate of Analysis is documentation that describes the results of product testing to determine the actual potency or amount of CBD and, when applicable, THC in the product. Legitimate manufacturers run these tests as part of their product quality assurance and make the COA available upon

request. (Contact the company directly with your request either by way of their website or using the contact information on their product label.)

The COA will also list significant amounts of any other ingredients, including other cannabinoids, and any potential allergens or contaminants. One of the most significant pieces of information you can take away from a COA is whether the lab meets ISO 17025 standards of testing. These are considered the high-bar standard and reputable labs use them as a baseline. Legitimate medical cannabis companies will readily advertise or make available their COA upon request to their sales or customer service representatives.

2. Check Labels

Although not required by law at this time, suppliers are increasingly listing the actual amount of CBD on the label or at least the percentage of CBD to other ingredients. This is helpful but not necessarily an ironclad reassurance of what you're buying. Several studies have found that products claiming on the label to contain CBD actually have only trace amounts. That's why the COA can be such a valuable tool to consumers. Another good sign on the label is the notification that the product has been tested in a third-party lab.

3. Buy American

Experts generally consider domestic hemp sources more reliable than foreign sources. That's because there are currently no regulations on how foreign-source hemp is grown, processed, or tested prior to importation. *Consumer Reports* recommends buying only from states that have legalized cannabis because those states are more likely to have regulations on the books that control the quality and claims made around hemp-derived CBD (and other cannabinoids).[82] For instance, they limit the type of pesticides that can be used on the plant because the plant is grown solely for consumption purposes.

4. Buy the Right Hemp Product

CBD extracted from hemp should come from the flowers and foliage of the plant, *not* the stems and seeds. The actual plant source of the CBD in the products you're considering buying should be made clear by the manufacturer. If it is not, you need to do some investigation to determine the source. If you can't find that information, I'd recommend

---

82. Lee Ceasrine and Rachel Rabkin Peachman, "6 Tips for Safe CBD Use," *Consumer Reports*, September 7, 2018, https://www.consumerreports.org/cbd/safe-cbd-use/.

considering another product. Keep in mind that if the label states "hempseed oil," any CBD will likely only be trace amounts and most likely none. The two terms are not interchangeable.

Last, as with any ingestible or beauty product, be skeptical of overblown marketing claims. The CBD product marketplace is crowded and growing right now. The easy way for companies to distinguish their products is to oversell benefits. A natural anti-inflammatory property might be embellished to become an "advanced wrinkle fighter."

Read labels closer than you do marketing materials and advertising, ask questions until you're confident you have all the information you need to make a wise and informed choice, and be critical of any statement not grounded in scientific reality.

Know Your CBD Terms

- CO_2 extraction. This is one way to isolate CBD out of plant material. High-pressure carbon dioxide (sometimes in tandem with other chemicals) is used in place of more caustic solvents to separate CBD from its plant source. CO_2 extraction can be used to collect other cannabinoids and terpenes in addition to the CBD.

  CBD is also extracted using olive oil, although this process yields less CBD. It is, however, just as safe as CO2 extraction. Dry-ice extraction is sometimes used as a low-cost alternative to CO2 extraction, but it generally produces a lower-quality CBD oil. Solvent extraction is a quick and inexpensive method that has been widely used. However, because it often employs highly toxic chemicals such as butane, it is not a preferred method and most medical marijuana practitioners strongly advise against using CBD oil extracted using solvents or other powerful chemicals.

- Hempseed oil. Because CBD is most commonly extracted from hemp, many consumers think hempseed oil and CBD products are interchangeable. They are not. Hempseed oil does not contain significant or any amounts of CBD. It is, however, a wonderful adjunct or partner to CBD or as a health ingredient on its own. In fact, many companies are producing hempseed oil skincare products because the oil contains high amounts of antioxidants, omega fatty acids, and a full range of vitamins. A 2014 article in *Pharmacognosy Reviews* suggested that the bioactive compounds in hempseed oil may actually strengthen the structure of skin, helping it ward off diseases and infection. The article's authors proposed that hempseed oil would be especially effective in treatment of

psoriasis, eczema, lichen planus, and acne rosacea.[83]
The oil also has beneficial anti-inflammatory properties and may play a small role in cardiovascular
and brain health.

- Full spectrum. This term is preferable to "isolated"
  (ISO) or "distillated" in relation to CBD. It means
  that the CBD was extracted along with other cannabinoids and even small amounts of THC. (In states
  where THC is illegal, look for CBD products labeled
  "broad spectrum," a term synonymous with "full
  spectrum," but more explicitly defined as not containing THC.) Products labeled with "pure" CBD
  can lead to confusion. Pure, in this case, means the
  CBD has been isolated from other, potentially beneficial, cannabinoids. The further CBD gets from
  its plant source, the more diluted the benefits of the
  CBD.

- Organic. As with other foodstuffs, any CBD labeled
  organic means the hemp was grown and processed
  without chemicals such as pesticides, chemical fertilizers, or solvents.

---

83. Nahida Tabassum and Mariya Hamdani, "Plants Used to Treat
Skin Diseases," *Pharmacognosy Reviews* 8, no. 15 (January–June
2014): 52–60, https://www.ncbi.nlm.nih.gov/pmc/articles
/PMC3931201/.

Other Concerns

If you're taking ingestible forms of CBD—specifically capsules—pay attention to the carrier medium used in the product. CBD is best transported into the body by a carrier oil containing medium-chain triglycerides. The most common is coconut oil. These types of carrier are easier for the body to process, making for a more complete and efficient use of the CBD by the body.

Of course, there is also the issue of expense. It's not necessarily beneficial, or even desirable, to replace all your skincare products with formulations containing CBD. If you're only looking for general health benefit, a daily moisturizer containing a significant percentage of CBD may be the only product you need to use. The truth is, in this early stage of CBD's introduction to the marketplace, any product with the cannabinoid is going to cost more than the same product without. Coupling a CBD moisturizer with your usual sunscreen and beauty products most likely will offer just as much benefit as switching all of your products to CBD versions.

Beyond Buying

You've checked the label, shopped different sources, investigated the manufacturer, even read the COA. You've checked with your doctor as necessary, and you've been a smart customer and bought a quality product. But all that is irrelevant if you don't use the product correctly.

The first step I would recommend anyone looking to treat any condition with CBD is to consult with his or her physician. The best-case scenario would be that your doctor has done coursework on medical marijuana. But even if he or she hasn't, you should inform your physician that you're considering using a cannabinoid. Any doctor will have the resources to keep any eye out for prescription drug interactions and other contraindications that might preclude CBD use, but your doctor can't provide the advice if you don't inform him or her.

Once you've purchased a topical formulation, ingestible forms of CBD, or both, using them consistently is key to getting the most benefit for your money. Do not stop and start usage with CBD or any other supplement. Decide on the proper dosage, and then take or apply it on a regular schedule (taking a brief few days off every few months). Only by standardizing the use of CBD can you measure its effectiveness and adjust accordingly.

Buy a reputable product in the ideal form for the condition you're treating, use it on a schedule that makes sense, and CBD can offer tremendous benefits to your skin and beyond.

The Future of CBD

The key to understanding the role CBD can play in your health and well-being is that, like any high-profile health compound, information is subject to change very quickly. Not only is the marketplace evolving, a greater number of states, and possibly even the federal government, may eventually legalize cannabis. This could lead to a wider range of CBD studies and uncover potential applications. I expect that the next few years will produce some eye-opening research results as well.

But one thing is certain: the potential and promise inherent in this compound is undeniable. I deeply believe that whether you're addressing a specific condition or just fine-tuning your skincare regimen, CBD has a role to play. Otherwise, I wouldn't have written this book.

The educated consumer and patient will be rewarded to one degree or another. I urge you to keep abreast of research and developments regarding CBD. As new findings are unveiled, we'll gain a better idea of just how this wonderful, natural tool can serve your skin and the rest of you. Here's to looking and feeling your best with the power of CBD!

RESOURCES

American Academy of Dermatology
Turn to the AAD for information on skin diseases and available treatments, proper care guidance for skin (and nails and hair, too), and even the chance to post a question and have it answered by a board-certified dermatologist.

www.aad.org

American Academy of Cannabinoid Medicine
This medical and scientific organization is focused on promoting ethical and practical standards for clinical applications of cannabis and cannabinoids. Its mission includes educating both professionals and the public on medical and scientific uses for the plant and its derived compounds.

www.aacmsite.org

American Epilepsy Society

This advocacy organization has set up a page dedicated to discussing how medical marijuana and CBD impact the fight against the disease (the first CBD-based epilepsy drug, Epidiolex was approved by the FDA in 2018).

https://www.aesnet.org/clinical_resources/medical%20 marjuana

American Herbal Pharmacopoeia

Advancing the goal of ensuring and promoting the responsible use of herbal medicines, the AHP produces many publications on different medicinal herbs and related issues. Although these monographs are meant as reference for doctors, researchers, and other professionals, they can also be used by the educated or intellectually curious lay person.

www.herbal-ahp.org

Americans for Safe Access

Dedicated to advancing research and the use of medical marijuana, ASA provides up-to-the-minute information on legal issues, therapeutic breakthroughs, and research on medical marijuana and related issues such as cannabinoid use.

www.safeaccessnow.org

Campaign for Safe Cosmetics

The CSC's goal is simple: pressure cosmetic companies to exclude hazardous chemicals and compounds from their products. The website gathers the latest news in safe personal care product development along with practical information and guidance on finding, buying, and using the safest cosmetic products possible.

www.safecosmetics.org

Center for Medicinal Cannabis Research

Established and funded by the California State Legislature, the Center is dedicated to promoting quality research and general understanding of the medicinal and therapeutic uses for cannabis. In addition to ongoing research, the CMCR also posts updates to federal policy positions on issues related to medical cannabis.

www.cmcr.ucsd.edu

Environmental Working Group
(Skin Deep Program)

The EWG's Skin Deep database provides practical advice for consumers to protect themselves from overexposure to chemicals. The Skin Deep database contains a list of personal care product profiles including dangers and health concerns.

www.ewg.org/skindeep

International Association for Cannabinoid Medicines

The IACM is a global organization dedicated to advancing knowledge of cannabis, cannabinoids, and the endocannabinoid system to explore and develop the therapeutic potential in medical cannabis. This site expands on the information presented in other websites listed here, because it includes study results and breaking information from around the globe.

www.cannabis-med.org

The International Cannabinoid Research Society (ICRS)

The ICRS serves as a hub of latest research and information on cannabinoids and all related topics, including regulation of the ECS, therapeutic and medical applications, and the abuse of marijuana. The site is meant primarily as a forum for scientists and other professionals to share information. Individuals can monitor the site and guide their practitioners to relevant studies that appear there.

www.icrs.co

Melanoma Research Foundation

This organization provides the latest information in the fight against the deadliest form of skin cancer. The organization is focused on aiding melanoma patients, survivors, and caregivers.

www.melanoma.org

National Weather Service UV Index
You can pop onto the website to regularly check how strong the UV rays are in your region, or download the available smartphone app for even more convenience. Either way, the index provides a guide to when you should exercise even more caution in protecting your skin (check out the explanations and recommendations on the website).

www.weather.gov/rah/uv

NIH National Center for Complementary and Integrative Health
This subdepartment of the National Institutes of Health does not focus solely on medical cannabis, but it does cover the topic at length, including research, news, and more.

www.nccih.nih.gov/health/marijuana

Project CBD
This is a non-profit educational news service providing soup-to-nuts information on CBD uses, latest research,

and medicinal applications and potential. The site includes references to other resources.

www.projectcbd.org

U.S. Department of Agriculture's National Organic Program
The National Organic Program maintains a list of certified organic growers and companies that you can consult to verify product claims. They also provide accreditation to producers and handlers or organic materials.

www.ams.usda.gov

Skin Cancer Foundation
This non-profit offers copious advice for both prevention and treatment of skin cancers. The website includes product recommendations, updates on the latest research, and more.

www.skincancer.org

BIBLIOGRAPHY

Abel, Ernest L. *Marihuana: The First Twelve Thousand Years*. New York: Springer Science + Business Media, 1980. First published 1943 by Plenum Press (New York).

Abotaleb, Mariam, Samson Mathews Samuel, Elizabeth Varghese, Sharon Varghese, Peter Kubatka, Alena Liskova, and Dietrich Büsselberg. "Flavonoids in Cancer and Apoptosis." *Cancers* 11, no. 1 (January 2019): 28. https://doi.org/10.3390/cancers11010028.

Ahn, Jiyun, Hyunjung Lee, Suna Kim, Jaeho Park, and Taeyoul Ha. "The Anti-obesity Effect of Quercetin Is Mediated by the AMPK and MAPK Signaling Pathways." *Biochemical and Biophysical Research Communications* 373, no. 4

(September 2008): 545–49. https://doi.org/10.1016/j.bbrc.2008.06.077.

Alshaarawy, Omayma, and James C. Anthony. "Are Cannabis Users Less Likely to Gain Weight? Results From a National 3-Year Prospective Study." *International Journal of Epidemiology* 48, no. 5 (October 2019): 1695–1700. https://doi.org/10.1093/ije/dyz044.

Appendino, Giovanni, Simon Gibbons, Anna Giana, Alberto Pagani, Gianpaolo Grassi, Michael Stavri, Eileen Smith, and M. Mukhlesur Rahman. "Antibacterial Cannabinoids from *Cannabis sativa*: A Structure-Activity Study." *Journal of Natural Products* 71, no. 8 (August 2008): 1427–30. https://doi.org/10.1021/np8002673.

Bergamaschi, Mateus Machado, Regina Helena Costa Queiroz, Antonio Waldo Zuardi, and Jose Alexandre S. Crippa. "Safety and Side Effects of Cannabidiol, A *Cannabis sativa* Constituent." *Current Drug Safety* 6, no. 4 (September 2011): 237–49. https://doi.org/10.2174/157488611798280924.

Birt, Diane F., Jill C. Pelling, Lenora T. White, Kaye Dimitroff, and Tracy Barnett. "Influence of Diet and Calorie Restriction on the Initiation and Promotion of Skin Carcinogenesis in the Sencar Mouse Model." *Cancer Research* 51, no. 7 (April 1991):

1851–54. https://cancerres.aacrjournals.org/content/canres/51/7/1851.full.pdf.

Boehnke, Kevin F., Evangelos Litinas, and Daniel J. Clauw. "Medical Cannabis Use is Associated with Decreased Opiate Medication Use in a Retrospective Cross-Sectional Survey of Patients with Chronic Pain." *The Journal of Pain* 17, no. 6 (June 2016): 739–44. https://doi.org/10.1016/j.jpain.2016.03.002;

Bonn-Miller, Marcel O., Mallory J. E. Loflin, and Brian F. Thomas. "Labeling Accuracy of Cannabidiol Extracts Sold Online." *JAMA* 318, no. 17 (November 2017): 1708–09. https://doi.org/10.1001/jama.2017.11909.

Booth, Martin. *Cannabis: A History.* New York: Thomas Dunne Books, 2004.

Bourrie, Mark. *Hemp: A Short History of the Most Misunderstood Plant and Its Uses and Abuses.* Buffalo, NY: Firefly Books, 2003.

Bremmer, Samuel, Abby S. Van Voorhees, Sylvia Hsu, Neil J. Korman, Mark G. Lebwohl, Melodie Young, Bruce F. Bebo Jr., and Andrew Blauvelt. "Obesity and Psoriasis: From the Medical Board of the National Psoriasis Foundation." *Journal of the American Academy of Dermatology* 63, no. 6 (December 2010): 1058–69. https://doi.org/10.1016/j.jaad.2009.09.053.

Burstein, Sumner. "Cannabidiol (CBD) and Its Analogs: A Review of Their Effects on Inflammation." *Bioorganic & Medicinal Chemistry* 23, no. 7 (April 2015): 1377–85. https://doi.org/10.1016/j.bmc.2015.01.059.

Caltagirone, Sara, Cosmo Rossi, Andreina Poggi, Franco O. Ranelletti, Pier Giorgio Natali, Mauro Brunetti, Francesca B. Aiello, Mauro Piantelli. "Flavonoids Apigenin and Quercetin Inhibit Melanoma Growth and Metastatic Potential." *International Journal of Cancer* 87, no. 4 (July 2000): 595–600. https://doi.org/10.1002/1097-0215(20000815)87:4<595::AID-IJC21>3.0.CO;2-5.

Cartwright, Mark. "Paper in Ancient China." Ancient History Encyclopedia. September 15, 2017. https://www.ancient.eu/article/1120/paper-in-ancient-china/.

Ceasrine, Lee and Rachel Rabkin Peachman. "6 Tips for Safe CBD Use." Consumer Reports. September 7, 2018. https://www.consumerreports.org/cbd/safe-cbd-use/.

Chaudhary, S. C., M. S. Siddiqui, M. Athar, M. Sarwar Alam. "d-Limonene Modulates Inflammation, Oxidative Stress and Ras-ERK Pathway to Inhibit Murine Skin Tumorigenesis." *Human & Experimental Toxicology* 31, no. 8 (February 2012): 798–811. https://doi.org/10.1177/0960327111434948.

Cheng, Yujie, Sha Liu, and Zhi Dong. "β-Caryophyllene Ameliorates the Alzheimer-like Phenotype in APP/PS1 Mice Through CB2 Receptor Activation and the PPARγ Pathway." *Pharmacology* 94, no. 1–2 (September 2014): 1–12. https://doi.org/10.1159/000362689.

Chye, Yann, Erynn Christensen, Nadia Solowij, and Murat Yücel. "The Endocannabinoid System and Cannabidiol's Promise for the Treatment of Substance Use Disorder." *Frontiers in Psychiatry* 10, no. 63 (February 2019): n.p. https://doi.org/10.3389/fpsyt.2019.00063.

Clarke, Robert C., and Mark D. Merlin. *Cannabis: Evolution and Ethnobotany.* Berkeley, CA: University of California Press, 2013. First published 1953 by University of California Press (Berkeley, CA).

Dariš, Barbara, Mojca Tancer Verboten, Željko Knez, and Polonca Ferk. "Cannabinoids in Cancer Treatment: Therapeutic Potential and Legislation." *The Bosnian Journal of Basic Medical Sciences* 19, no. 1 (February 2019). 14–23, https://doi.org/10.17305/bjbms.2018.3532.

Duncan, Bruce B., Maria Inês Schmidt, James S. Pankow, Christie M. Ballantyne, David Couper, Alvaro Vigo, Ron Hoogeveen, Aaron R. Folsom, and Gerardo Heiss. "Low-Grade Systemic Inflammation and the Development of Type 2 Diabetes." *Diabetes* 52, no. 7 (July 2003): 1799–805, https://doi.org/10.2337/diabetes.52.7.1799.

Eagleston, Lauren R. M., Nazanin Kalani, Ravi Rajendra Patel, Hania K. Flaten, Cory A. Dunnick, and Robert P. Dellavalle. "Cannabinoids in Dermatology: A Scoping Review." *Dermatology Online Journal* 24, no. 6 (June 2018): 1–17. https://www.semanticscholar.org/paper/Cannabinoids-in-dermatology%3A-a-scoping-review.-Eagleston-Kalani/0f25c04e84ec93462a83e6541fd3a878643e8aa1.

Expert Committee on Drug Dependence. *Cannabidiol (CBD) Pre-Review Report, Agenda Item 5.2, Thirty-ninth Meeting* (Geneva, Switzerland: World Health Organization, November 2017): 1–27. https://www.who.int/medicines/access/controlled-substances/5.2_CBD.pdf.

Fan, Dongsheng, Xin Zhou, Chao Zhao, Huaguo Chen, Yang Zhao, and Xiaojian Gong. "Anti-inflammatory, Antiviral and Quantitative Study of Quercetin-3-O-β-D-Glucuronide in *Polygonum perfoliatum* L." *Fitoterapia* 82, no. 6 (September 2011): 805–10. https://doi.org/10.1016/j.fitote.2011.04.007.

Fidyt, Klaudyna, Anna Fiedorowicz, Leon Strządała, and Antoni Szumny. "β-caryophyllene and β-caryophyllene Oxide—Natural Compounds of Anticancer and Analgesic Properties." *Cancer Medicine* 5, no. 10 (October 2016): 3007–17. https://doi.org/10.1002/cam4.816.

Fuss, Johannes, Jörg Steinle, Laura Bindila, Matthias K. Auer, Hartmut Kirchherr, Beat Lutz, and Peter Gass. "A Runner's High Depends on Cannabinoid Receptors in Mice." *Proceedings of the National Academy of Sciences of the United States of America* 112, no. 42 (October 2015): 13105–108. https://doi.org/10.1073/pnas.1514996112.

Giacoppo, Sabrina, and Emanuela Mazzon. "Can Cannabinoids be a Potential Therapeutic Tool in Amyotrophic Lateral Sclerosis?" *Neural Regeneration Research* 11, no. 12 (December 2016): 1896–99. https://doi.org/10.4103/1673-5374.197125.

Gonzalez-Cuevas, Gustavo, Remi Martin-Fardon, Tony M. Kerr, David G. Stouffer, Loren H. Parsons, Dana C. Hammell, Stan L. Banks, Audra L. Stinchcomb, and Friedbert Weiss. "Unique Treatment Potential of Cannabidiol for the Prevention of Relapse to Drug Use: Preclinical Proof of Principle." *Neuropsychopharmacology* 43, no. 10 (September 2018): 2036–45. https://doi.org/10.1038/s41386-018-0050-8.

De Hertog, Sofie A. E., Christianne A. H. Wensveen, Maarten T. Bastiaens, Christine J. Kielich, Marjo J. P. Berkhout, Rudi G. J. Westendorp, Bert J. Vermeer, and Jan N. Bouwes Bavinck. "Relation Between Smoking and Skin Cancer." *Journal of Clinical Oncology* 19, no.

1 (January 2001): 231–38. https://doi.org/10.1200/
JCO.2001.19.1.231.

Huestis, Marilyn A. "Human Cannabinoid Pharmacokinetics." *Chemistry & Biodiversity* 4, no. 8 (August 2007):
1770–1804. https://doi.org/10.1002/cbdv.200790152.

Hemp Farming Act of 2018. H.R.5485, 115th Cong., 2nd
sess., *Congressional Record* 165 (July 25, 2019), HR 5485.

Kim, Hyun Jong, Bongwoo Kim, Bu Man Park, Jeong
Eun Jeon, Sin Hee Lee, Shivtaj Mann, Sung Ku Ahn,
Seung-Phil Hong, Se Kyoo Jeong. "Topical Canna-
binoid Receptor 1 Agonist Attenuates the Cutane-
ous Inflammatory Responses in Oxazolone-Induced
Atopic Dermatitis Model." *International Journal of
Dermatology* 54, no. 10 (October 2015): 401–08.
https://doi.org/10.1111/ijd.12841.

Konieczny, Eileen, and Lauren Wilson. *Healing with
CBD: How Cannabidiol Can Transform Your Health
Without the High*. Berkeley, CA: Ulysses Press, 2018.

Lafaye, Genevieve, Laurent Karila, Lisa Blecha, and
Amine Benyamina. "Cannabis, Cannabinoids, and
Health." *Dialogues in Clinical Neuroscience* 19, no. 3
(September 2017): 309–16. https://www.ncbi.nlm.nih.
gov/pmc/articles/PMC5741114/.

Latek, Tom. "Hemp Manufacturer GenCanna Teams
with UK Researchers, Says They Have a Material with

Zero THC." *Northern Kentucky Tribune.* Kentucky Center for Public Service Journalism. January 30, 2019. https://www.nkytribune.com/2019/01/hemp-manufacturer-gencanna-teams-with-uk-researchers-says-they-have-a-material-with-zero-thc/.

Legault, Jean, Wivecke Dahl, Eric Debiton, André Pichette, and Jean-Claude Madelmont. "Antitumor Activity of Balsam Fir Oil: Production of Reactive Oxygen Species Induced by alpha-Humulene as Possible Mechanism of Action." *Planta Medica* 69, no. 5 (May 2003): 402–07. https://doi.org/10.1055/s-2003-39695.

Leinow, Leonard, and Juliana Birnbaum. *CBD: A Patient's Guide to Medical Cannabis.* Berkeley, CA: North Atlantic Books, 2017.

Liput, Daniel J., Dana C. Hammell, Audra L. Stinchcomb, and Kimberly Nixon. "Transdermal Delivery of Cannabidiol Attenuates Binge Alcohol-Induced Neurodegeneration in a Rodent Model of an Alcohol Use Disorder." *Pharmacology Biochemistry and Behavior* 111 (October 2013): 120–27. https://doi.org/10.1016/j.pbb.2013.08.013.

Liu, Yong, Anne G. Wheaton, Daniel P. Chapman, Timothy J. Cunningham, Hua Lu, and Janet B. Croft. "Prevalence of Healthy Sleep Duration among Adults—United States, 2014." *Morbidity and Mortality*

Weekly Report Centers for Disease Control and Prevention 65, no. 6 (February 2016): 137–41. http://dx.doi.org/10.15585/mmwr.mm6506a1.

Loflin, Mallory J. E., Kimberly A. Babson, and Marcel O. Bonn-Miller. "Cannabinoids as Therapeutic for PTSD." *Current Opinion in Psychology* 14 (April 2017): 78–83. https://doi.org/10.1016/j.copsyc.2016.12.001.

Lu, Xiao-Guang, Li-Bin Zhan, Bing-An Feng, Ming-Yang Qu, Li-Hua Yu, and Ji-Hong Xie. "Inhibition of Growth and Metastasis of Human Gastric Cancer Implanted in Nude Mice by d-Limonene." *World Journal of Gastroenterology* 10, no. 14 (July 2004): 2140–44. https://www.ncbi.nlm.nih.gov/pmc/articles/PMC4572353/.

Machowska, Anna, Juan Jesus Carrero, Bengt Lindholm, Peter Stenvinkel. "Therapeutics Targeting Persistent Inflammation in Chronic Kidney Disease." *Translational Research* 167, no. 1 (January 2016): 204–13. https://doi.org/10.1016/j.trsl.2015.06.012.

Maida, Vincent, and Jason Corban. "Topical Medical Cannabis: A New Treatment for Wound Pain—Three Cases of Pyoderma Gangrenosum." *Journal of Pain and Symptom Management* 54, no. 5 (November 2017): 732–36. https://doi.org/10.1016/j.jpainsymman.2017.06.005.

Morena, Maria, Sachin Patel, Jaideep S. Bains, and Matthew N. Hill. "Neurobiological Interactions between Stress and the Endocannabinoid System." *Neuropsychopharmacology* 41, no. 1 (January 2016): 80–102. https://doi.org/10.1038/npp.2015.166.

Moskowitz, Michael H. *Medical Cannabis: A Guide for Patients, Practitioners, and Caregivers*. Virginia Beach, VA: Köehler Books, 2017.

Murata, Soichiro, Risa Shiragami, Chihiro Kosugi, Tohru Tezuka, Masato Yamazaki, Atsushi Hirano, Yukino Yoshimura, et al. "Antitumor Effect of 1, 8-cineole Against Colon Cancer." *Oncology Reports* 30, no. 6 (December 2013): 2647–52. https://doi.org/10.3892/or.2013.2763.

Nallathambi, Rameshprabu, Moran Mazuz, Aurel Ion, Gopinath Selvaraj, Smadar Weininger, Marcelo Fridlender, and Ahmad Nasser, et al. "Anti-Inflammatory Activity in Colon Models Is Derived from Δ^9-Tetrahydrocannabinolic Acid That Interacts with Additional Compounds in *Cannabis* Extracts," *Cannabis and Cannabinoid Research* 2, no. 1 (2017): 167–182. https://www.ncbi.nlm.nih.gov/pubmed/29082314.

Newton, David. *Marijuana: A Reference Handbook*. 2nd ed. Santa Barbara, CA: ABC-CLIO, 2017.

Oláh, Attila, Balázs I. Tóth, István Borbíró, Koji Suga-
    wara, Attila G. Szöllősi, Gabriella Czifra, Balázs Pál, et
    al. "Cannabidiol Exerts Sebostatic and Antiinflamma-
    tory Effects on Human Sebocytes." *Journal of Clinical
    Investigation* 124, no. 9 (September 2014): 3713–24.
    https://doi.org/10.1172/JCI64628.

Park, Hye Min, Eunjung Moon, Ae-Jung Kim, Mi Hyun
    Kim, Sanghee Lee, Jung Bok Lee, Yong Kon Park,
    Hyuk-Sang Jung, Yoon-Bum Kim, Sun Yeou Kim.
    "Extract of *Punica granatum* Inhibits Skin Photoaging
    Induced by UVB Irradiation." *International Journal of
    Dermatology* 49, no. 3 (March 2010): 276–82. https://
    doi.org/10.1111/j.1365-4632.2009.04269.x.

Parray, Hilal Ahmad, and Jong Won Yun. "Cannabidiol
    Promotes Browning in 3T3-L1 Adipocytes." *Molecu-
    lar and Cellular Biochemistry* 416, 1–2 (May 2016):
    131–39. https://doi.org/10.1007/s11010-016-2702-5.

Perucca, Emilio. "Cannabinoids in the Treatment of
    Epilepsy: Hard Evidence at Last?" *Journal of Epilepsy
    Research* 7, no. 2 (December 2017): 61–76. https://
    www.ncbi.nlm.nih.gov/pmc/articles/PMC5767
    492/.

Śledziński, Paweł, Joanna Zeyland, Ryszard Słomski, and
    Agnieszka Nowak. "The Current State and Future Per-
    spectives of Cannabinoids in Cancer Biology." *Cancer

Medicine 7, no. 3 (March 2018): 765–75. https://doi.org/10.1002/cam4.1312.

Reiman, Amanda, Mark Welty, and Perry Solomon. "Cannabis as a Substitute for Opioid-Based Pain Medication: Patient Self-Report." *Cannabis and Cannabinoid Research* 2, no. 1 (June 2017): 160–66. https://doi.org/10.1089/can.2017.0012;

Rogerio, A. P., A. Kanashiro, C. Fontanari, E. V. G. da Silva, Y. M. Lucisano-Valim, E. G. Soares, and L. H. Faccioli. "Anti-inflammatory Activity of Quercetin and Iso-quercitrin in Experimental Murine Allergic Asthma." *Inflammation Research* 56, no. 10 (October 2007): 402–08. https://doi.org/10.1007/s00011-007-7005-6.

Russo, Ethan, Geoffrey Guy, and Philip Robson. "Cannabis, Pain, and Sleep: Lessons From Therapeutic Clinical Trials of Sativex®, a Cannabis-Based Medicine." *Chemistry & Biodiversity* 4, no. 8 (August 2007): 1729–43. https://doi.org/10.1002/cbdv.200790150.

Sabogal-Guáqueta, Angélica Maria, Edison Osorio, and Gloria Patricia Cardona-Gómez. "Linalool Reverses Neuropathological and Behavioral Impairments In Old Triple Transgenic Alzheimer's Mice." *Neuro-pharmacology* 102 (March 2016): 111–20. https://doi.org/10.1016/j.neuropharm.2015.11.002.

Setty, Arathi R., Gary Curhan, and Hyon K.Choi. "Smoking and the Risk of Psoriasis in Women: Nurses'

Health Study II." *The American Journal of Medicine* 120, no. 11 (November 2007): 953–59. https://doi.org/10.1016/j.amjmed.2007.06.020.

Shannon, Scott, Nicole Lewis, Heather Lee, and Shannon Hughes. "Cannabidiol in Anxiety and Sleep: A Large Case Series." *The Permanente Journal* 23 (2019): n.p. https://doi.org/10.7812/TPP/18-041.

Simmerman, Erika, Xu Qin, Jack C. Yu, and Babak Baban. "Cannabinoids as a Potential New and Novel Treatment for Melanoma: A Pilot Study in a Murine Model." *Journal of Surgical Research* 235 (March 2019): 210–15. https://doi.org/10.1016/j.jss.2018.08.055.

Swenson, Ben. "Hemp & Flax in Colonial America." *The Colonial Williamsburg Journal* (Winter 2015). https://www.history.org/Foundation/journal/Winter15/hemp.cfm.

Tabassum, Nahida and Mariya Hamdani. "Plants Used to Treat Skin Diseases." *Pharmacognosy Reviews* 8, no. 15 (January–June 2014): 52–60. https://www.ncbi.nlm.nih.gov/pmc/articles/PMC3931201/.

Tóth, Kinga Fanni, Dorottya Ádám, Tamás Biró, and Attila Oláh. "Cannabinoid Signaling in the Skin: Therapeutic Potential of the 'C(ut)annabinoid' System." *Molecules* 24, no. 5 (March 2019): 918. https://doi.org/10.3390/molecules24050918.

Tubaro, Aurelia, Anna Giangaspero, Silvio Sosa, Roberto Negri, Gianpoalo Grassi, Salvatore Casano, Roberto Della Loggia, and Giovanni Appendino. "Comparative Topical Anti-inflammatory Activity of Cannabinoids and Cannabivarins." *Fitoterapia* 81, no. 7 (October 2010): 816–19. https://doi.org/10.1016/j.fitote.2010.04.009.

Turner, Helen, Daniel Chueh, Tony Ortiz, Alexander J. Stokes, and Andrea L. Small-Howard. "Cannabinoid Therapeutics in Parkinson's Disease: Promise and Paradox." *Journal of Herbs, Spices & Medicinal Plants* 3 (2017): 231–248. https://doi.org/10.1080/10496475.2017.1312724.

WHO Expert Committee on Drug Dependence, Fortieth Report. WHO Technical Report Series No. 1013 (Geneva, Switzerland: World Health Organization, 2018): ii–49. https://apps.who.int/iris/bitstream/handle/10665/279948/9789241210225-eng.pdf?ua=1.

Yang, Zhiwei, Nan Wu, Yuangang Zu, and Yujie Fu. "Comparative Anti-Infectious Bronchitis Virus (IBV) Activity of (-)-Pinene: Effect on Nucleocapsid (N) Protein." *Molecules* 16, no. 2 (February 2011): 1044–54. https://doi.org/10.3390/molecules16021044.

Yu, Xiao, Hongyan Lin, Yu Wang, Wenwen Lv, Shuo Zhang, Ying Qian, Xiaobei Deng, Nannan Feng, Herbert Yu, and Biyun Qian. "d-Limonene Exhibits

Antitumor Activity by Inducing Autophagy and Apoptosis in Lung Cancer." *Onco Targets and Therapy* 11 (April 2018): 1833–47. https://doi.org/10.2147/OTT.S155716.

Wargent, Edward T., Mohamed Zaibi, Cristoforo Silvestri, David C. Hislop, C. J. Stocker, Colin Stott, Geoffrey W. Guy, Marnie Duncan, Vincenzo Di Marzo, and Michael Cawthorne. "The Cannabinoid Δ9-tetrahydrocannabivarin (THCV) Ameliorates Insulin Sensitivity in Two Mouse Models of Obesity." *Nutrition & Diabetes* 3, e68 (2013): n.p. https://doi.org/10.1038/nutd.2013.9.

Weydt, Patrick, Soyon Hong, Anke Witting, Thomas Möller, Nephi Stella, and Michel Kliot. "Cannabinol Delays Symptom Onset in SOD1 (G93A) Transgenic Mice Without Affecting Survival." *Amyotrophic Lateral Sclerosis and Frontotemporal Degeneration* 6, no. 3 (September 2005): 182–84. https://doi.org/10.1080/14660820510030149.

Wilson, Brummitte Dale, Summer Moon, and Frank Armstrong. "Comprehensive Review of Ultraviolet Radiation and the Current Status on Sunscreens." *The Journal of Clinical and Aesthetic Dermatology* 5, no. 9 (September 2012): 18–23. https://www.ncbi.nlm.nih.gov/pmc/articles/PMC3460660/.

To Write to the Author

If you wish to contact the author or would like more information about this book, please write to the author in care of Llewellyn Worldwide Ltd. and we will forward your request. Both the author and publisher appreciate hearing from you and learning of your enjoyment of this book and how it has helped you. Llewellyn Worldwide Ltd. cannot guarantee that every letter written to the author can be answered, but all will be forwarded. Please write to:

Manisha Singal, MD
℅ Llewellyn Worldwide
2143 Wooddale Drive
Woodbury, MN 55125-2989

Please enclose a self-addressed stamped envelope for reply,
or $1.00 to cover costs. If outside the U.S.A., enclose
an international postal reply coupon.

Many of Llewellyn's authors have websites with additional information and resources. For more information, please visit our website at http://www.llewellyn.com